Your Positive Mindset Playbook

Praise for *Your Positive Mindset Playbook*

"Sully is one of the most dedicated, disciplined, and positive people I've ever had the pleasure to work with! That combination undoubtedly is a primary catalyst for his consistently high performance for so many years. *Your Positive Mindset Playbook* is filled with wisdom he has gained from real life experiences – I plan to share it with my entire team!"

—**Liz Moore,** Owner, Liz Moore & Associates

"All of us face professional challenges, and those in the real estate industry face them every day whether it's a bad market, difficult clients, difficult transactions, etc. Such challenges are inevitable but succumbing to them is optional. As long as I have known Sully, which is a long time indeed, he has always chosen not to surrender. And his positive mindset has to be the reason!"

—**Brian D. Lytle,** Esq.

"Robert Sullivan has an excellent understanding of what it means to shift from negative automatic thought processes to having a positive mindset. *Your Positive Mindset Playbook* is a wonderful application tool that will encourage others to recognize and overcome their own mindset challenges."

—**Dasmier Mason,** LPC

"As the CEO of the Virginia Peninsula Association of Realtors, I have witnessed Sully's leadership skills for years. His positive mindset is infectious and people flock to work alongside him. For those of you who feel stuck in life right now, this playbook is a must read."

—**James Wetzell,** CEO, Virginia Peninsula Association of Realtors

"When one has a positive mindset, it renews your spirit as Sully notes in this publication. When your spirit is renewed, it allows clarity of mind and energy in your body. This powerful combination provides both peace and a gateway to success. Sully has long served as a stellar example of positive mindset, and I am fortunate to count him as a great mentor. May the words of *Your Positive Mindset Playbook* bless everyone who reads them."

—**Kaera Mims, President,** Virginia Peninsula Association of Realtors

"How totally appropriate for Sully to have written *Your Positive Mindset Playbook*. He is the purest example of how to embrace your faith in the everyday "practice" of joy, through mindset. He has been a mentor and friend for over 15 years – his beautiful energy is contagious. I am thrilled he is now sharing this gift with the world."

—**Ginny Phillips,** Senior Mortgage Banker

YOUR
POSITIVE
MINDSET
PLAYBOOK

100 DAYS TO A BETTER LIFE

ROBERT "SULLY"
SULLIVAN

NEW YORK

LONDON • NASHVILLE • MELBOURNE • VANCOUVER

Your Positive Mindset Playbook

100 Days to a Better Life

Published in New York, New York, by Morgan James Publishing. Morgan James is a trademark of Morgan James, LLC. www.MorganJamesPublishing.com

Proudly distributed by Ingram Publisher Services.

Morgan James BOGO™

A **FREE** ebook edition is available for you or a friend with the purchase of this print book.

CLEARLY SIGN YOUR NAME ABOVE

Instructions to claim your free ebook edition:
1. Visit MorganJamesBOGO.com
2. Sign your name CLEARLY in the space above
3. Complete the form and submit a photo of this entire page
4. You or your friend can download the ebook to your preferred device

ISBN 9781636980881 paperback
ISBN 9781636980898 ebook
Library of Congress Control Number:
2022948623

Cover Design by:
Chris Treccani
www.3dogcreative.net

Cover Concept by:
Kathy Sturgeon

Interior Design by:
Christopher Kirk
www.GFSstudio.com

Morgan James PUBLISHING Builds with... **Habitat for Humanity** Peninsula and Greater Williamsburg

Morgan James is a proud partner of Habitat for Humanity Peninsula and Greater Williamsburg. Partners in building since 2006.

Get involved today! Visit: www.morgan-james-publishing.com/giving-back

To Teresa, my bride and my soulmate. Since we married in 1999, you have consistently inspired me to become a better man, and a better person.

CONTENTS

PREFACE

Many years ago, I would show up for work at seven o'clock and start my day by reading motivational, uplifting material, and then writing positive affirmations about what I read. The material I read ranged from business publications to Scripture. A typical Monday through Friday meant five to ten daily written affirmations.

After about a dozen years, for some unknown reason, I stopped this daily routine. Don't get me wrong, I still read, but what I read was the daily newspaper, online news sites, and online sports sites. Slowly but surely, without me even recognizing what was happening, my mindset shifted from one of joy and optimism to one of anxiety and worry. In fact, on a couple of occasions, I went into deep depressions. I thank God, Teresa, and my pastor for helping me through those dark times.

Then it hit me. I had stopped filling my mind with positivity and replaced it with negativity.

That is what propelled me to write this book. If you too are feeling anxious, overwhelmed, and depressed, and you aren't sure why, perhaps you are like me and could use some more positivity in your life to outweigh the negativity.

During my time as a United States Air Force officer, we read *The Art of War* by Sun Tzu. He stated it was important to know your enemy. Sometimes we are own worst enemy, and if we know ourselves, we can "overcome" ourselves to be the best we can be. We will never be perfect, but we can always be growing and improving, particularly in the area of mental health.

Having written literally thousands of affirmations over the years, I chose my top one hundred and decided to write about each one individually and what they mean to me. Some ideas or metaphors may overlap with others, but that is intentional. Sometimes it takes hearing something several times before it actually sinks in.

This book is designed as a workbook. We learn when we read, but we learn more when we write and contemplate what we read and/or wrote. After each affirmation, there is a lined page. On the first three lines, you can rewrite the affirmation for that day three times. On the remaining lines, you can write what that affirmation means to you personally, even if it has no meaning to you at the moment. At the very least, you have opened yourself to receive more positivity in your life.

May you always fill your mind with uplifting thoughts, and may your words to yourself and others be encouraging. Be well, and happy thinking!

Day 1

I renew my spirit and mindset every day.

Back in the mid-1990s, Mike Ferry, a national real estate coach/trainer, introduced me and the hundreds of others at his seminar to the power of affirmations. It was a way to keep us motivated through the ups and downs of our industry. Every morning I would show up at the office prior to anyone else being there and read uplifting material from various authors. From the material I read, I would handwrite ten or more affirmations per day. Over the years, as I developed spiritually, I added reading/studying the Bible to my daily routine with the goal to read the Bible cover to cover every year. This book is a culmination of my reading and writing of affirmations.

I do not know why, but I stopped reading uplifting material. I started reading the local newspaper and online stories from national news sites. The result was a gradual, downward spiral into depression. I was married to the love of my life, healthy, no real financial worries, and here I was . . . depressed.

It dawned on me to go back to the basics. I stopped receiving the daily paper, would only glance at news headlines to keep informed, and went back to reading motivational material, secular and spiritual. I *need* to renew my spirit and mindset every day. If I do not, the world will invade it.

It is paramount that we renew our spirit and our mindset every day, even when we are on cloud nine. Renewing our spirit and mindset daily will keep us from even peering into that rabbit hole. Mr. Ferry does not know me, but thanks, Mike.

Rewrite the affirmation three times:

1. _____

2. _____

3. _____

Personal thoughts:

_____

_____

_____

_____

_____

_____

_____

_____

_____

_____

Day 2

I am at peace with imperfection.

Have you ever replied to an email, and by the time you click the "send" button, forty-five minutes have passed, you have edited and re-edited more than a dozen times—and it was only a four-sentence reply?

Or have you ever put on an outfit, liked the way it looked and made you feel, but still changed your outfit three more times before ultimately deciding you were ready to go?

Trying to be perfect can result from a variety of reasons, including not liking to be criticized or critiqued (who does?), the need to seek praise and admiration, or even using perfection in one area as an excuse to avoid doing something else at that moment. The fact is, trying to be perfect can literally rob you of precious time and add a heaping dose of stress into your life.

This does not mean settling for "good enough," or doing just enough to get by on any task. We are not here to settle for mediocrity. What we're talking about is when the result is not worth the extra effort it takes to achieve that result. Perhaps the moment before you decided that *great* was not "good enough" truly was . . . *good enough.*

If you find yourself in a situation where something is great but you believe it can be better, take a step back and objectively look at the situation. What is a better use of your time and energies: getting something perfect (if that's even possible), getting another project started, or perhaps just taking time to relax and breathe?

Rewrite the affirmation three times:

1. _____

2. _____

3. _____

Personal thoughts:

_____

_____

_____

_____

_____

_____

_____

_____

_____

_____

Day 3

I remind myself daily of the person I wish to be.

Let's face it; we all wish to be better than we are in at least some aspect of our lives. For some, we wish we were a better spouse or a better parent. For others, it could be healthier, wealthier, or wiser. The question comes down to, "Then why aren't we?" If we truly desire to be these things, what is preventing us?

The answer is simple: *Life* is preventing us from achieving or becoming the above. I remember hearing Zig Ziglar once say, "You become what you think about." That is huge. As we go about our day, we do *not* think about becoming a better spouse or parent or becoming healthier, wealthier, or wiser. We are too trapped in merely getting through the day.

The true secret to becoming whatever it is you desire is to think about it often. This does not mean to risk getting fired from your job for daydreaming. It involves keeping whatever it is that you desire to be always or somewhere near your consciousness. When you take time to dwell on something, the most powerful computer in the world, *your brain*, will figure out a way to make it happen. If you truly desire to become a better spouse and you contemplate regularly on this, thoughts of flowers, love notes, romance, or acts of kindness will come into your mind. Then it just becomes a matter of acting on these ideas.

Remind yourself *daily* of who or what you desire to be or have. Then do not be surprised when you find yourself accomplishing whatever it is that you have been thinking about.

Rewrite the affirmation three times:

1. _____

2. _____

3. _____

Personal thoughts:

_____

_____

_____

_____

_____

_____

_____

_____

_____

Day 4

I know that today's challenges will be tomorrow's history.

I f you are reading this, you have experienced challenges in your life, many of them in fact. Some challenges might have been self-inflicted, while other challenges were thrust upon you and you had no control over them. Yet, you still had to overcome them. Challenges materialize in every facet of your life, including relationships, finances, health, professional endeavors, etc.

Right now, take a few minutes and remember back to some challenges you faced in the past. Chances are you remember only a tiny fraction of those challenges. If you were able to time-travel back to when you were faced with these challenges, you most likely would see yourself all worked up and thinking how insurmountable these challenges were.

The point here is that at this present moment, you have both knowledge and hope. Your knowledge stems from the fact that regardless of the challenges you faced in the past, they are over and done with and probably have little to no impact on you today.

With this knowledge comes hope. You can now deal with a challenge today with the knowledge that in the future, you will look back at this challenge knowing you overcame it. This knowledge provides you with hope, and with hope comes joy.

So, face today's challenge knowing that this too shall pass. It might not be today or tomorrow, but soon today's challenge will be history.

Rewrite the affirmation three times:

1. _____

2. _____

3. _____

Personal thoughts:

_____

_____

_____

_____

_____

_____

_____

_____

_____

_____

Day 5

I realize the power of my own thoughts.

This is arguably the most important affirmation that you will ever repeat to yourself. This affirmation, when fully believed, embraced, and repeated daily, has the power to make *every* day a great day.

Whenever he is asked about his day, my friend Kevin always replies, "Best day ever!" At first I thought this was a bit corny. But then I started to play back the conversations we'd had in the past and paid attention to our current conversations. He never seemed to get flustered about any situation that he was currently dealing with, and some situations were extraordinarily serious.

It was at this time that I fully realized the power of this affirmation. When something was going bad in my life and I focused on the negative aspects of whatever was going on, I remained in a bad mood, lost sleep, and continuously replayed the negativity in my mind. At times, I was miserable.

When I shifted gears in my thought process from all the negativity I was experiencing and started thinking about what I could learn, how I could be a blessing to someone, etc., my day and disposition brightened tremendously.

I encourage you to fully embrace the power your thoughts have not only on you, but on everyone around you. The next time you start a negative thought process, make a conscious decision to turn those thoughts around and see how it changes your attitude. Make it, "The best day ever!"

Rewrite the affirmation three times:

1. _____

2. _____

3. _____

Personal thoughts:

_____

_____

_____

_____

_____

_____

_____

_____

_____

Day 6

I know my success starts the moment I do.

It must be stated that success is different for everybody. For some, success is defined by family and/or relationships, for others it is spiritually oriented; however, many others think success follows the old axiom, "He [or she] who dies with the most toys, wins." Regardless of how you personally define success, arguably the two largest obstacles to a person achieving success are procrastination and complacency.

Within your definition of success, look around and see who is successful in a way that mirrors your definition. Chances are they did not become that successful over night; in fact, it most likely took them years of trial and error to achieve that level of success. If you dream of being that successful, it will begin the moment you begin. You must decide to act on it *today* and not tomorrow. Guaranteed, if you wait until tomorrow to act, something *will* pop up that will cause you to say, "I'll act tomorrow." Procrastination is one of two killers to anyone's success.

The other is complacency. Please understand, if you are okay with your life right now, that is perfectly fine. Your definition for success might be exactly where you are right now. Not everyone is wired to constantly seek to achieve more. However, if you feel like you need a change in some area of your life, I strongly urge you to find someone else *today* who is excelling in that area and set up a time to meet with them. Pick their brains and glean a nugget . . . *today.*

Rewrite the affirmation three times:

1. _____

2. _____

3. _____

Personal thoughts:

_____

_____

_____

_____

_____

_____

_____

_____

_____

_____

Day 7

I always work ten minutes more when I feel like quitting.

How about a little math to start? There are fifty-two weeks in a year, and let's assume we have two weeks off for vacation, illness, or whatever. That leaves us with fifty weeks in the year for productivity. This productivity can be in any area of your life, from fitness to finances to spirituality. Now within those fifty weeks, we have five "work" days; let's call them Monday through Friday. This equates to 250 "work" days. If you were to work just ten minutes more per day in any area that you desire an improvement, that would equate to 2,500 more minutes spent on whatever it is you chose to be better in. Those 2,500 more minutes equate to almost forty-two more hours of productivity, just by putting in ten more minutes of effort.

Now, for example, let's take fitness. For a person who exercises five days per week, what do you think an extra forty-two hours of working out will do for them in a year? What about your relationships? What do you think an extra forty-two hours of devotion per year toward a loved one will do? What about your spirituality? What spiritual fruit could be borne in your life if you spent an extra forty-two hours in devotion toward God?

Ten minutes more in any facet of your life will yield huge results. In what area in your life would you like to see a huge, positive change, and are you willing to indulge an extra ten minutes per day toward that goal? Even if you are at zero time spent right now, imagine what an extra forty-two hours spent in that area will do for you this time next year. Don't stop . . . just ten minutes more! You can do it!

Rewrite the affirmation three times:

1. _____

2. _____

3. _____

Personal thoughts:

_____

_____

_____

_____

_____

_____

_____

_____

_____

Day 8

I am willing to start at the beginning.

We all must start somewhere. Even the oak started from the acorn. The problem many of us face is that we want to start our adult lives as the fully mature, mighty oak. We live in a world of immediacy. Fast food, same-day delivery of online purchases, instant everything. We want it all and we want it right now—and why not, if it is available?

I distinctly remember being in my early twenties as a new college graduate. I wanted the lifestyle of my parents immediately. It never occurred to me that they spent fifty-plus years of hard work and experiencing their own trials and tribulations to get to that point. So what did I do? I attempted to circumvent the system and have their lifestyle by going into debt, which took me years to recover from.

None of us want to experience the trials and tribulations that come from time and experiences. On a professional level, we want the same success as the person who has been with the company for twenty years. On a personal level, we want the same relationship as the thirty-plus years of the happily married couple.

But picture the mighty oak. First that acorn had to break apart and a seedling had to emerge. Then that seedling had to face and survive droughts, floods, storms, being chopped down, and more. Eventually, it grew and grew into the mighty oak. That is what we must be willing to endure, and if we do, in time, we too will be the mighty oak standing tall and standing strong.

Rewrite the affirmation three times:

1. _____

2. _____

3. _____

Personal thoughts:

_____

_____

_____

_____

_____

_____

_____

_____

_____

_____

Day 9

I know that triumph lies in discipline.

T here probably is not a more true or accurate statement in this whole book. Name one facet of your life where this does not apply. What I would like for you to do right now is imagine yourself being more disciplined in an area of your life that needs improving, and then project yourself six months down the road.

In the area of health, if you were more disciplined in terms of what you put into your body and exercise, how do you see yourself six months from now? If you were more disciplined in how you accrued income and how you spent your money, how would your financial picture look six months from now? How about your relationships? Face it! Being in a relationship takes work and discipline. If you were disciplined enough to act toward your partner the same way you did when you first met, how would that relationship be six months from now?

This is easier said than done because discipline usually involves discomfort if not outright pain. You will absolutely feel like you are being tried by fire. But you know what? Pure gold is tried by fire. It is put through intense fire and the impurities are driven out, leaving pure gold. This is what discipline will do for every facet of your life.

My question to you is this: Are you ready to discipline yourself to make changes that will dramatically improve the quality of your life, or do you need to hit rock bottom first?

Rewrite the affirmation three times:

1. _____

2. _____

3. _____

Personal thoughts:

_____

_____

_____

_____

_____

_____

_____

_____

_____

_____

Day 10

I give myself the freedom to fail.

Outside of the other four-letter word that begins with F, *fail* is perhaps one of the ugliest words we ever hope to hear about ourselves. In school, getting that big red capital F, perhaps with a circle drawn around it, was the mark of humiliation. It indicated you were less than everyone else in the class who scored better, and even more horrific, it meant the wrath of your parents.

So we have all been brainwashed into thinking failures are bad! This could not be further from the truth. The truth of the matter is that MOST failures are good if not great because they get us one step closer to success. The only caveat to this, of course, is that we keep on trying and learning from our failures until eventually success unfolds like a glorious ocean sunrise on a cloudless morning.

Think about it. Science is arguably 99 percent about failure. This is what the scientific method is all about. Try something, log the results, and try again doing something a little differently. Where would our space program, medicine, or even athletics be without failure every step of the way? Do you realize that a Hall of Fame professional baseball player who bats .300 for his career fails to get a hit 70 percent of the time? And yet this qualifies him to be among the best of the best.

Knowing this, why are we so afraid to fail? The answer is because we personally identify with failure and see ourselves *as* failures. I challenge you today to intentionally fail at something and then take notice around you. The sun still rises, and it will still set. Be bold!

Rewrite the affirmation three times:

1. _____

2. _____

3. _____

Personal thoughts:

_____

_____

_____

_____

_____

_____

_____

_____

_____

_____

Day 11

If I find myself in a hole, I stop digging.

Guilty as charged for outright laughing as I typed this affirmation. The problem with my laughing is I am not sure if I'm laughing because the affirmation is inherently funny or because I have needlessly dug many a hole for myself.

Isn't it interesting that when reading this affirmation, we automatically think of someone else who this would apply to . . . but certainly not to ourselves? It is so easy for us to see the hole others are digging, and we also have a good visual of the shovel they are using to dig that hole. To us, it seems as simple as removing that shovel (whatever they are doing to create a bigger hole for themselves) from their hands and their lives would start to get better.

But what about our own holes? What shovel are we using to dig our hole deeper? In our relationships, could that shovel take the form of self-absorption? In our finances, could that shovel be a lack of a strong work ethic or self-discipline in our spending habits? What about our health? Do our shovels take the form of poor eating habits or lack of exercise?

Whatever hole you find yourself in, I strongly urge you to identify your shovel. What is causing you to go deeper into the hole? When you figure it out, get the help you need to remove that shovel from your hands. If you are religiously inclined, God's Word is there to help. If you're not, surely there is someone you know who will gladly help take away your shovel. Stop digging!

Rewrite the affirmation three times:

1. _____

2. _____

3. _____

Personal thoughts:

_____

_____

_____

_____

_____

_____

_____

_____

_____

_____

Day 12

I row when there is no wind.

Sailing through life: Isn't that everyone's desire? Regardless of where we are in life right now, there have been seasons where we have indeed sailed through life. In fact, the wind was so strong at our backs that outside of steering the ship, we did little to move forward on our own. Life was good, there were no worries, and everything was falling into place.

But we all know that those seasons are rare and short-lived. For most of us, either the wind has completely died down or, worse, it is blowing against us. What then?

The easy thing to do would be to set anchor and just sit, knowing that you'll no longer be moving forward and hoping you don't drift backwards. Here is where the desire and strength of personal goals come into play. If your goals are powerful enough, you will desire to continue moving forward, even if that means getting out your oars and rowing.

As you row through life, you must know that it will be tiresome at times, and your human tendency will be to quit and rest. Your brain will do some amazing rationalization to justify quitting rowing. At this point I urge you to keep rowing, even if at a slower pace. If you quit and regress, you will now have to cover the same ground that you lost twice, and who wants to do that? Keep rowing, people, and know that the wind will soon be at your back again.

Rewrite the affirmation three times:

1. _____

2. _____

3. _____

Personal thoughts:

_____

_____

_____

_____

_____

_____

_____

_____

_____

_____

Day 13

I reach for the stars to keep my hands out of the mud.

This affirmation provides a spectacular visualization. Just by reading this affirmation, can you see yourself reaching high up into the heavens, while also ignoring the mud all around you?

Close your eyes and picture this if you will. It is a glorious, clear sky, the air is crisp, and you are away from the city where the twinkling lights of the stars are innumerable. Now picture those stars to be the vision of what you dream your life could and should be. Finally, I want you to picture a hand reaching down from the stars, grasping your hand firmly, albeit gently, and pulling you up into the stars (your dreams) until you are among them. How awesome is this? Smiling yet?

Conversely, picture yourself standing next to a lake of mud whose depth is unknown to you. You reach down into the mud until just your elbow is showing, when suddenly you feel something once again firmly, but this time violently, pulling your whole body down into the muck and mire. A horror story, no doubt!

The point is, if you reach for your dreams, there will be people there to help pull you into the stars. Likewise, and I promise, if you choose to immerse yourself in the mud of this world, someone will help pull you in deeper as well. The choice to reach where you want is purely yours, but I exhort you to reach for the stars.

Rewrite the affirmation three times:

1. _____

2. _____

3. _____

Personal thoughts:

_____

_____

_____

_____

_____

_____

_____

_____

_____

_____

Day 14

I have given up my past so I can live my future.

Holding on to our past will surely keep us from creating the future we deserve. Maybe we are holding on to something terrible that happened to us back then, physically or mentally, that prevents us from achieving what we desire today and for our future. It could be some sort of abuse, an accident or illness, the environment we grew up in, or pretty much anything.

But holding onto your past doesn't always equate to something negative. It could also be referring to "the good ole days." A classic example of this is the Bruce Springsteen song, "Glory Days." The song is about two high school friends who meet up later in life, go into a bar to have a drink, and one of them can't stop talking about the glory days of high school baseball. In the meantime, life is passing him by in that very moment.

Look at your current life. Are you using your past as an excuse not to create the future you desire? Are you saying you cannot have a better life because of something bad that happened years ago? Or are you on the other side of the spectrum and saying you cannot have as good of a life as you had back then, so why bother?

If you feel that you may be in this kind of situation (perhaps without even realizing it), I encourage you to seek help either professionally or from those positive people in your life who love and care for you. Find some way to give up and release your past so you can live the future you desire. The choice is yours.

Rewrite the affirmation three times:

1. _____

2. _____

3. _____

Personal thoughts:

_____

_____

_____

_____

_____

_____

_____

_____

_____

Day 15

I focus on the people I am talking to.

Have you ever been engaged in a conversation with someone and their eyes are wandering all over the place except where they need to be, focused on you? How about talking to someone who is scrolling through social media or emails on their phones? How do you feel about that?

Recently I had a one-on-one conversation with the owner of our company. Obviously, she is well above me on the food chain, so to speak. What I distinctly remember about our conversation is that she looked me directly in the eye while we were talking, said my name organically a couple of times in the conversation, and then asked genuine questions, showing she was fully engaged in that moment.

I was absolutely blown away by this. Even though she must have had thousands of other more important things to do and people to see, she made me feel like the most important person to her. I walked away from that conversation feeling wonderful.

I am sure you have had similar experiences, both with a person who was not present in the moment and a person who was totally focused on you, even if it was just for five minutes. I encourage you to become like the owner of our company. Note, this will take practice and concentration, both to remain this focused but also to make it feel natural for both you and the people you are speaking to. The rewards will be worth it, I promise.

Rewrite the affirmation three times:

1. _____

2. _____

3. _____

Personal thoughts:

_____

_____

_____

_____

_____

_____

_____

_____

_____

_____

Day 16

I choose great people to be around.

My son Greg asked me to be his best man at his and Melissa's wedding. One of the duties of the best man is to give a toast at the reception. I had all sorts of anecdotes about Greg, some humorous and some poignant, about his and my journey through life. Prior to the wedding, I was struck by the friends from his childhood who came to the celebration, some as far as 3,000 miles away.

Like a tsunami washing over me, I suddenly knew what my toast would be about. It would celebrate Greg and Melissa while at the same time encourage others. The toast was centered around the people Greg chose to surround himself with his entire life. He chose to hang with exceptional people on paths of achievement and service to others and, by doing so, created the foundation and support system for his own excellence in life. It is important to know that I did not choose Greg's friends; he chose them himself. My role, as his father, was to instill in him the importance of carefully choosing the people that surround you.

No matter your age or current situation, take note of the people around you. Are they inspiring you to live a better life, or are they enabling you to live a life you wish were not yours? This is not advice to jettison your current friends completely out of your life. Instead, it is advice to look for excellent people to add into your life. Over time, as your life evolves into the one you desire, the chaff of your life will be carried away and you will be left with golden wheat.

What will you do today to bring a person of excellence into your life, and what will you do to keep them there?

Rewrite the affirmation three times:

1. _____

2. _____

3. _____

Personal thoughts:

_____

_____

_____

_____

_____

_____

_____

_____

_____

_____

Day 17

I do not pursue happiness; I create it.

I t seems like everyone is chasing that one thing that, if they possess it, will make them happy. It could be a relationship, wealth, education, fame, etc. The fact of the matter is you can create your happiness at any time. I'm not saying to *not* pursue those things, but to pursue those things to supplement the current happiness you have already created.

As you know, I am a big fan of old sayings. Here's another one: "No matter where you go, you take yourself with you." If you are unhappy now, obtaining something that you think will make you happy will provide only fleeting happiness. Once the shininess of the new toy wears off, there you are, with yourself.

The key to a happy life is to be able to create happiness in any moment. But how do you do this? Focus on what you have right now. To create your happiness, it is as simple as focusing on what is good right now in your life instead of focusing on what is wrong. But don't just think about what is right—dwell on it. This is not a checklist. Take the time to appreciate and savor what is going well in your life.

Today, right now, think of one thing that is going right in your life and then meditate on that for a few minutes. Chances are when you are done, you will be smiling.

Don't pursue your happiness, create it!

Rewrite the affirmation three times:

1. _____

2. _____

3. _____

Personal thoughts:

_____

_____

_____

_____

_____

_____

_____

_____

_____

Day 18

I control my life; it is not on autopilot.

A common statement when someone's life is going well is that their life is on autopilot. Everything is going smoothly; they do not need to steer, provide power, etc. to get where they want to go.

The problem with having your life on autopilot is that unless you disengage the autopilot, you are no longer truly in control of your life. What if you wish to reach a goal more quickly? Or what if you wish to slow down and take advantage of a beautiful scenic overlook that presents a once-in-a-lifetime opportunity? Keeping to a strict autopilot mindset does not allow for either.

Another problem with autopilot is that it could cause you to fall asleep at the wheel of your life, so to speak. You won't be aware of potential "road hazards" that may need to be steered around. When your life is on autopilot, you tend to take things and people for granted and become oblivious to everything around you, and that leads to neglect. We all know that anything left neglected tends to decay and die. This could occur in our relationships, finances, health, spirituality, or whatever else is important to us.

I am not saying to never put your life on autopilot. It is a nice luxury and sometimes even a necessity to take a break. However, I highly encourage you to regularly disengage the autopilot and take control of your life, even if only for a short period of time.

Rewrite the affirmation three times:

1. _____

2. _____

3. _____

Personal thoughts:

_____

_____

_____

_____

_____

_____

_____

_____

_____

Day 19

I take time to review my daily habits and actions.

American writer Edgar Rice Burroughs once said, "People are creatures of habit." What does the word *habit* mean to you? Are habits a good thing? Perhaps. Are they bad? Maybe. Most likely, we all have both good and bad habits.

The problem with habits lies in the fact that, most often, we do not realize we have them. We go through our days, just trying to get through the day, and do not even realize how we got through that day. For example, when the alarm goes off in the morning, do you pop right out of bed, or do you keep hitting the snooze alarm until the last possible minute?

The successful person is going to spend some time working *on* their life versus spending all their time working *in* their life. Take some time on a regular basis to examine your routines. Break them up into morning, afternoon, and evening. While looking at your routines/habits, identify the ones that are good and empowering and identify the ones that are negative and limiting. If you are having a hard time getting to sleep at night, look at your habits right before trying to sleep. Are you engaged in electronics like television, phone, or social media? Perhaps this habit could be changed so that all of that is turned off an hour before bedtime and you use that time to read, pray, or meditate.

Review your daily habits and actions. Which ones are good and need reinforcing, and which ones do you consider to be negative? It is important to regularly study your daily habits to ensure your lifetime habits are supportive versus destructive.

Rewrite the affirmation three times:

1. _____

2. _____

3. _____

Personal thoughts:

_____

_____

_____

_____

_____

_____

_____

_____

_____

_____

Day 20

I work on my weaknesses instead of others' weaknesses.

This book is written for people of all worldviews, and the Bible can be a tremendous source of wisdom and knowledge regardless of your beliefs. For example, take the following verse from the Gospel of Matthew, which states, "Why do you look at the speck of sawdust in your brother's eye and pay no attention to the plank in your own eye? How can you say to your brother, 'Let me take the speck out of your eye, when all the time there is a plank in your own eye?' You hypocrite, first take the plank out of your own eye, and then you will see clearly to remove the speck from your brother's eye" (Matthew 7:3–5, NKJV).

Sadly, this affirmation and verse speak loudly to me, though I am trying hard to remove the plank(s) from my own eye. We often go through life seeing others' misfortunes and easily "know" why this is happening to them. We think, "It is so obvious as to why this is happening to them. Why don't they do this or change that?"

The problem with pointing a finger at someone else is that when we do this, there are *always* three fingers pointing straight back at ourselves. If you do not believe me, point your index finger at something and then notice which direction the remaining three fingers are pointing.

The next time you have the urge to point out someone else's weakness, take the time to recognize and work on your own. By making yourself a better person, you will be amazed how those around you suddenly start to improve themselves.

Rewrite the affirmation three times:

1. _____

2. _____

3. _____

Personal thoughts:

_____

_____

_____

_____

_____

_____

_____

_____

_____

_____

Day 21

I am the blacksmith of my life.

What an awesome visual! Picture a blacksmith in the Old West. Perhaps you envision a big, burly man, perhaps bearded, wearing a protective apron, using a hammer to forge hot metal by pounding the hot metal into shape on an anvil. When the hot metal cools, something that will last a lifetime has been created.

This is what we must do to create the life we desire. For most of us, our lives are like the cold metal to start. It is only when heat is applied that the metal (our lives) can begin to be softened, pounded, and shaped. Sadly, for most of us, the heat that is applied to our lives and necessitates the need for pounding and reshaping comes in the form of some sort of desperation. Perhaps we are in trouble with the law or have habits that wreak havoc on relationships, finances, or health.

The great news is that we do not have to reshape our lives because of some calamity. You can do this simply by having an extreme desire (applied heat to make your cold life more pliable) to change something in your life, and then by eliminating negative habits and replacing them with positive habits (the hammer), you create the life you desire. As you can imagine, being whacked with a hammer (replacing habits) can, and most likely will, be painful. But in the end, what you create will be a work of beauty—*your* work of beauty.

Take time today to think about an area in your life that you need to forge into something beautiful and better. Don't wait until calamity strikes to force the change; take it upon yourself to voluntarily become the blacksmith of your life.

Rewrite the affirmation three times:

1. _____

2. _____

3. _____

Personal thoughts:

_____

_____

_____

_____

_____

_____

_____

_____

_____

_____

Day 22

I have the power to choose so I also have the power to change.

We all have the power to choose basically anything that affects our lives. For example, we have the power to choose what we eat and drink. We have the power to choose what our eyes see on TV or social media. We have the power to choose what we listen to. Heck, we even have the power to choose our thoughts. Just because a thought enters our head doesn't mean we have to dance with it. We can choose to discard or replace that thought.

Having the power to choose gives us the power to change. If a person consumes two soft drinks per day, they ingest roughly 500 calories per day just from those soft drinks. If that person would eliminate just one soft drink, that equates to over 91,000 empty calories per year that are not ingested. What kind of change would happen in a person's life by consuming 91,000 fewer sugar calories?

You have the power to change your mood as well. Outside of depression, a very serious but treatable disease, most people are unhappy due directly to the thoughts they are dancing with in their minds. When a negative thought pops into our mind, we can choose not to entertain that thought and replace it with another more uplifting thought and dance with it instead. The more you choose to control the thoughts you dance with, the happier your life will be.

I encourage you to choose to replace just one *small* thing in your life with something more positive. What change do you think it will make for you?

Rewrite the affirmation three times:

1. _____

2. _____

3. _____

Personal thoughts:

_____

_____

_____

_____

_____

_____

_____

_____

_____

Day 23

I know personality opens doors, but character keeps them open.

Think back on your life. Have you ever met someone at school, work, or church that you were drawn to like a magnet? What drew you to them initially? It certainly wasn't their character because you don't know a person's character until you spend time with them. Was it their looks? Was it their humor? Was it their position in life? Was it their personality? It doesn't matter what draws you to someone initially; what matters is how you feel about a long-term relationship with them either personally or professionally. Are you excited about the possibility, or do you dread the thought?

What about us? Are people naturally drawn to us for our personality or for some other reason? Looking back, how many people have come and gone from our lives and how many have stuck around? How many of these people who are drawn to us could we count on to give a moving eulogy at our funeral?

It is important to have one or more traits that draw *good* people to us. Traits like kindness, professionalism, humor, spirituality; they are all good for initial connections. What is even more important is your character—it's what makes people want to stay around you and be your friend long after the newness of the relationship is over.

What is one of your personality traits that opens the door for new friendships? Looking at your life from an out-of-body perspective, how is your character? Will it allow new relationships to blossom into long-term relationships?

Rewrite the affirmation three times:

1. _____

2. _____

3. _____

Personal thoughts:

_____

_____

_____

_____

_____

_____

_____

_____

_____

_____

Day 24

I think through problems versus worry through problems.

Worry is *not* our friend! Let me repeat that. Worry is *not* our friend. I dare anyone to tell me one problem in the history of mankind that was resolved simply by worrying. All worrying does is contribute to stress (which is the number one cause of health issues in the world), and it prevents us from thinking through issues in a logical, well-thought-out fashion.

Not worrying about problems does not mean we should not be concerned about them. Worry is *concern* on steroids. When we worry, our mind automatically focuses on worst-case scenarios instead of solutions to problems. In fact, many times we worry about a problem that hasn't even materialized and may never materialize. We worry about something that "might" happen. Don't deny it, I know you have done this . . . at least you have if you're human.

Here is a little formula for preventing worry and thinking your way clearly through SOME problem, where SOME stands for Situation, Objective, Means, and Evaluation.

Situation: Write down the situation as it truly is, not how you think it may end up. If you cannot be objective about this, get someone to help you state the Situation clearly.

Objective: What is the outcome that you wish to achieve?

Means: What is the action plan that you will employ to achieve the Objective?

Evaluation: Did your Means accomplish your Objective?

When we logically think through our issues instead of worrying about them, in most cases, good things happen. The next time a problem arises, try SOMEthing different and see what happens.

Rewrite the affirmation three times:

1. _____

2. _____

3. _____

Personal thoughts:

_____

_____

_____

_____

_____

_____

_____

_____

_____

Day 25

I have taken charge of who I am.

O ne of the reasons I wrote this book is because I have periodic bouts with depression. It usually originates from the negativity or injustice that sometimes surrounds me or from smart people behaving in absolutely asinine ways, reaping the repercussions, and then saying, "Why didn't anyone tell me?" Where my problem lies is in not dealing with the onslaught of depression until it festers and worsens. Writing this book and completing the exercises it contains helps me not only keep my depression at bay, but stay joyful too.

It has taken me sixty-plus years of living by trial and error to realize that I must keep constant vigilance on who I am, who I am becoming, and who I desire to be. When I fail to keep this vigilance, the old me creeps back in, and he usually brings along a whole slew of nasty friends.

On a regular basis, and this could be anywhere from daily to monthly, I urge you to take stock of who you are, even if it is just a thirty-minute self-evaluation. How are you treating your relationships? Your finances? Your health? Do you need to make any adjustments? Far too often, we get so wrapped up in getting through the day-to-day aspect of our lives that we can go deep down the rabbit hole of negative habits.

Let's start now. Just like a person may take their car in for an annual inspection to see if it is running properly or if something needs attention before something else catastrophic happens, let's give our lives a bit of an inspection right this moment.

Rewrite the affirmation three times:

1. _____

2. _____

3. _____

Personal thoughts:

_____

_____

_____

_____

_____

_____

_____

_____

_____

_____

Day 26

I am creating enough evidence to be convicted of being kind.

What is the first thing that pops into your mind when you hear the word *convicted*? Because of the preponderance of news stories and TV shows dealing with crime, you most likely think of someone being led away in handcuffs after a judge or jury finds them guilty.

However, to be convicted of something simply means to be *certain* of something. It can also refer to your beliefs about what is right and what is wrong.

We must work to create enough evidence so the people around us are certain that we are kind. They judged us and found us guilty of kindness. If we work hard enough, perhaps that will be our legacy. How cool is that?

How do we get convicted of being kind? Again, as in most things, it comes down to mindset and planning. Have in your mind from the very start of your day that you are going to look for opportunities to be kind. If you do this, those opportunities will pop up and it will be up to you to respond. It could be something as simple as a smile or holding a door open. If no opportunity readily presents itself, look at the people around you. Tell one of them how much you appreciate them or note a specific trait about them that you appreciate.

Today, what evidence will you generate to help convict you of being kind?

Rewrite the affirmation three times:

1. _____

2. _____

3. _____

Personal thoughts:

_____

_____

_____

_____

_____

_____

_____

_____

_____

_____

Day 27

I have woken up and am paying attention.

"**W**ake up, people!" Boy, if I had a nickel for every time a teacher said that to my class growing up, or the ROTC drill instructors shouted it at the cadets at camp, I would be rich right now. Well, maybe not rich, but I would have at least a dollar more to my name. The point of their exclamation to *wake up* was that we were not paying attention to what was going on in the moment—we were just going through the motions. Sadly, there are people who sleepwalk like this through life.

Why do people sleepwalk through life? Obviously, I am not a doctor, but from my experience, I would say it boils down to two main issues. A person may be afflicted with one or, perhaps, both. First, depression is a real thing, and it is devastating to both the person afflicted by this very real disease and for the loving people around them. Secondly, some have no vision for their lives, so they put their life on autopilot and sleepwalk through their days, weeks, and years.

As I mentioned earlier, I this book as part of my own healing from depression. If you even think that you are depressed, please, please, please seek medical help. Depression is as destructive to a person as any other kind of disease, but it is treatable. The world has come a long way in reducing the stigma of depression. Except for a few Neanderthals walking around, no one tells a depressed person to just smile.

If you are not depressed but simply have no vision for your life . . . *wake up!* If you do not know how to create your vision or a plan to achieve it, find someone who does. Find a mentor and go through your day intentionally.

Rewrite the affirmation three times:

1. _____

2. _____

3. _____

Personal thoughts:

_____

_____

_____

_____

_____

_____

_____

_____

_____

_____

_____

Day 28

I know where I can make a difference, so I do.

This affirmation applies on so many levels, from personal to global. How did we get into the mindset of, if I can't do everything, I won't do anything?

In the global arena, there is no way that anyone can wipe out poverty, war, or disease on their own. But we all can do something, and if we all did something, no matter how big or small, wouldn't the cumulative effects be dramatic? We all have varying measures of available time, talent, and treasure. If you are super busy and cannot give of your time, a donation (treasure) would surely help. If you cannot afford to share your treasure as you struggle to make ends meet, perhaps you have time to give that would be helpful.

The personal arena has the same issues as the global arena. Have you ever tried to prepare a holiday dinner for twenty to thirty people? Most likely you could not do everything, but you did do what you could and hopefully the other people attending helped as well. Perhaps a guest was not able to provide a dish for the meal. Since they are attending the meal, maybe their "something" is to help with the cleanup. Even on a small level like this, you might not be able to do everything, but you can do something.

Today, look around your work environment as well as your home environment. Does someone or something need help? You may not be able to do everything for the situation, but you can do something. Maybe that something is to enlist the help of others who can do something as well.

Rewrite the affirmation three times:

1. _____

2. _____

3. _____

Personal thoughts:

_____

_____

_____

_____

_____

_____

_____

_____

_____

Day 29

I am a faithful steward of my resources.

A faithful steward is someone doing the best they can to care for whatever is in their possession. Most people think of resources from a monetary or materialistic perspective when in reality they are limitless. While our finances, vehicles, and residences are indeed resources, they are but a few that we possess. Our health is a resource. Our relationships are resources. Our faith is a resource. Everything in our lives is a resource that needs to be cared for and nurtured.

We abuse our resources by taking them for granted. When we treat these resources as if they will always be there or are easily replaceable, we become poor stewards. Divorces occur because one or both people do not nurture the relationship until it is irretrievably broken. Finances run afoul when we spend more than we make, thinking that we can always make more money.

We become faithful stewards when we take an active role in not only maintaining the resource but seeking to make it better. We are faithful stewards of our homes and cars by keeping them clean and performing the recommended periodic maintenance. We become faithful stewards of our marriages when we put the needs and desires of our spouse ahead of our own, not because we must but because we want to, just like when we were dating.

Look at the resources in your life. Are you being a faithful steward of them? Are you seeking to make them better or are they being taken for granted? Commit today to becoming a faithful steward of your resources.

Rewrite the affirmation three times:

1. _____

2. _____

3. _____

Personal thoughts:

_____

_____

_____

_____

_____

_____

_____

_____

_____

Day 30

I am specific when I offer to help.

In times of illness, heartache, or tragedy, we often hear, "Please let me know what I can do to help." I have been guilty of this on many occasions. For many people, this is a sincere statement, while for others it just seems like the polite thing to say.

Depending on the situation at hand, the person you are saying this to might be in such a jumbled state of mind that they literally cannot think of anything at that moment, even though there may be dozens of ways you could help. Their natural response to your statement is a sincere and polite, "Thank you."

A better way to offer to help is to be specific. If the situation requires a large gathering, perhaps you can offer to make meals, enough to feed everyone, along with the accompanying paper products needed. Or if they are going to be having out-of-the-area visitors, offer to pick them up at the airport or host them in your spare bedroom(s). Could you help with lawn care? Do the children need to be taken to any activities or appointments? There are myriad ways that we can be specific in our offer to help. When we are specific, the person we are offering to help can focus on what your offer is instead of trying to reply with a mind that may be, at best, foggy.

The next time an opportunity to help someone presents itself, instead of providing a generalized offer, examine the person and situation and see if there is something specific you could do to help. It will be much more appreciated and, more than likely, accepted.

Rewrite the affirmation three times:

1. _____

2. _____

3. _____

Personal thoughts:

_____

_____

_____

_____

_____

_____

_____

_____

_____

_____

Day 31

I am content with my surroundings but not with myself.

For some people, the word *content* means to be satisfied with where they are in life, while for others it is as loathsome a word as can be imagined. Because the Bible references the need to be content, many people use it as an excuse to remain stagnant in their life. That is not what the Bible says. The Bible teaches that we should not favor material possessions over our relationship with God. In fact, the Bible says we should continually strive to become *more* Christ-like, aka to *not* be content with who we are right now.

What I am affirming here is that while it is okay to be fine with the material things around us, we should never be content with who we are as individuals. Shouldn't we all strive to be better spouses? Better parents? Better employees or employers? Better friends? This is what it means to not be content with ourselves. When we better ourselves, everything around us gets swept along with that tidal wave of improvement and our surroundings improve as well.

A professor of mine once said that she will stop learning and stop teaching on the day she takes her last breath. What a testament to not being content with one's self. We should all seek to modify that statement to say, "We will stop growing and improving on the day we take our last breath."

While it is okay to be content with our surroundings, we must strive to never be content with ourselves. What part of *you* will you make better today?

Rewrite the affirmation three times:

1. _____

2. _____

3. _____

Personal thoughts:

_____

_____

_____

_____

_____

_____

_____

_____

_____

Day 32

I have the confidence to live without all the answers.

What are you most confident in? Is it your abilities? Do you place your confidence in someone else or something else? Is trust equal to confidence? Does a lack of confidence hurt your state of mind? Does it create worry?

Our experiences absolutely confirm that some questions simply have no answers. And yet we will beat ourselves up in a continuous quest for answers that will never be found. To make matters worse, we *know* these answers will not be found and yet we still seek them.

Why? We seek answers in the hope that all will be revealed and provide us with peace of mind. We would like to say, "Aha! So that is why this happened." People ask, "Why do bad things happen to good people?" Would the answer, assuming one does exist, change the situation? No, it would not.

Also, would knowing the answers to our burning questions suddenly make our lives all rainbows and butterflies? It would not. Many people talk about a need for closure. Closure is not going to change the situation or make life better.

Knowing the answers to our questions is not going to change the situation or make life instantly better. We must live with confidence and trust that it is okay to live without all the answers.

Rewrite the affirmation three times:

1. _____

2. _____

3. _____

Personal thoughts:

_____

_____

_____

_____

_____

_____

_____

_____

_____

Day 33

I realize that I only have one chance at this very moment.

L et's do a little exercise. Right now, look at the time to include seconds, if possible, and remember it. Now close your eyes and count to one hundred at a normal speed, and then look at the time again. How much actual time passed by?

Here is a thought for us to ponder: the time that passed by can never be regained. Let that sink in. It is gone forever. Now, expand that time scenario to an hour, a day, a week, and a year. It is a stark realization that as each second, day, week, month, or year passes by, it is time we can never get back.

What could we have accomplished during that lost time? How could we have used that time to make our lives or the life of someone else better? I am not saying that every second of every day must be productive. Rest is extremely important for a quality life and perhaps exactly what was needed at the time.

Communication technology and entertainment are two of the greatest tools to building quality lives, and, arguably, they are two of the biggest roadblocks to building quality lives. Look at the amount of time people spend on their computers, phones, etc., or plopped in front of a TV screen. That is time they will never get back. While most things are great in moderation, we must be cognizant of how we spend our time.

A quality life begins when we realize we only have one chance at this very moment. How will you spend it?

Rewrite the affirmation three times:

1. _____

2. _____

3. _____

Personal thoughts:

_____

_____

_____

_____

_____

_____

_____

_____

_____

Day 34

I embrace pressure as it turns coal into diamonds.

Technically speaking, there is no scientific proof that diamonds are made from coal. Though they are both made from carbon, coal is produced much closer to the surface of the earth than are diamonds. But it makes for a great analogy, so we will continue in that vein . . . pun indeed intended.

Just as fire removes impurities from gold, pressure and time change coal into diamonds. However, not only are diamonds one of the most valuable gemstones in the world, but they are also one of the hardest elements on the earth. They are frequently used in tools for cutting, drilling, and grinding.

When we are under pressure, depending on how we control our mindset, we too are refined. When we successfully endure a situation applying pressure in our lives, we become, over time, more valuable to the world and to those around us. Furthermore, we become even stronger and more able to endure future pressure.

Pressure in the shape of obstacles, deadlines, financial worries, relationship issues, and so forth will impact our lives at some point. We must learn to embrace them, weather through them, and come out better in the end. Liz Moore, the owner of one of the most successful boutique real estate firms in the industry, often would tell us, "Learn to embrace the challenges inherent in our industry, for without them, our clients would not need us. Be the hero in every transaction."

Whatever pressure you face today, embrace it, and become a precious diamond.

Rewrite the affirmation three times:

1. _____

2. _____

3. _____

Personal thoughts:

_____

_____

_____

_____

_____

_____

_____

_____

_____

_____

Day 35

I have stopped the negative chatter in my brain.

My mind used to be filled with, and sometimes still deviates to, negative chatter. One of our adult children would do something unwise, by any standard, and my mind would obsess with it for days on end. Or a client would act in a greedy or unfair manner, and my mind would ask over and over why someone could act this way toward another human. And do not get me started on politics.

Chatter is nothing more than incessant talk about trivial matters. Let's break that down. *Incessant* is something that continues without pause. Unless my mind was occupied with something else, these trivial matters would continue without pause. I am intentionally using the word *trivial* because more times than not it *was* inconsequential, and, in my mind, I was blowing it all out of proportion.

All this negative chatter was, at best, purposeless, pessimistic, and unpleasant. There was *never* a time when I finished a good ole negative chatter session where I left in a joyful frame of mind. And yet I continued to engage until I discovered in my research how this was destroying my life. Unless I took control of the negative chatter in my brain, I would be one short step away from depression.

We all are going to host negative chatter sessions in our brain from time to time. One key secret to living a more joyful life is to recognize either the triggers that set the session in motion, or to recognize when we have entered that session. With that recognition, we are then equipped to stop the session and move on. Be well!

Rewrite the affirmation three times:

1. _____

2. _____

3. _____

Personal thoughts:

_____

_____

_____

_____

_____

_____

_____

_____

_____

Day 36

I seek to be the lit candle in a dark room.

The world can be a dark place. From terrorism to crime to the actions of our political leaders, doom and gloom are all around. Closer to home, based on what is happening in our immediate surroundings, we might be in our own dark room. Our personal dark rooms take the shape of lost loved ones and financial, employment, and health issues, to name a few.

We can be the lit candle that provides light/hope, no matter how small, to that dark room. There is a Chinese proverb that states, "It is better to light a candle than to curse the darkness." This means that instead of being sad about something, be a beacon of hope, be the lit candle. If the candle is lit, no room can be completely dark.

If we are that lit candle of hope, it becomes extremely important to take care of the candle too so it does not burn out. The lit candle is our mindset and how we communicate with others. Are we filling our minds with fuel to keep the candle lit, or are we filling it with things that will extinguish the flame? When we talk to others, are our words uplifting, or do they bring us and others down into the darkness? One of the best attributes of a lit candle is that it can be used to light other candles. Think about it. Your beacon of hope can spread to others and so on down the line. After a while, instead of a dark room, the whole room is filled with light, and it all started with one lit candle.

Today, whatever dark room you find yourself in, seek to be that lit candle.

Rewrite the affirmation three times:

1. _____

2. _____

3. _____

Personal thoughts:

_____

_____

_____

_____

_____

_____

_____

_____

_____

_____

Day 37

I seek out ways to praise and encourage others.

One would think that the most important part of this affirmation is the praise and encouragement of others. While that is significant, the most important point of this affirmation is the action of *seeking out*.

When we seek out ways to praise and encourage others, we become intentional. Unlike seeing someone and giving them a spontaneous compliment, when we are intentional, there is a thought process, a planning process involved. This thought process of seeking out ways to praise and encourage others automatically puts our brains in a positive frame of mind. When our brain becomes intentionally positive, it touches all the other areas of our lives as well. While we know the act of praise and encouragement helps others, it benefits us even more.

The obvious person who benefits from praise is the person to whom the praise and encouragement are given. No matter what is going on in their lives in the moment, either good or bad, you have just lifted them up, made them feel valued, and thus made them feel better. Praise and encouragement reinforce whatever initiated the encouragement in the first place. This positive reinforcement will spur the desire to continue in similar fashion.

Today, think of someone you think could use a little praise and encouragement. Perhaps it is a child, a parent (yes, parents need encouragement too), or maybe the person in the cubicle across the aisle. *Seek out* ways to praise and encourage this person. You *both* will reap the rewards, I promise.

Rewrite the affirmation three times:

1. _____

2. _____

3. _____

Personal thoughts:

_____

_____

_____

_____

_____

_____

_____

_____

_____

Day 38

I work hard to protect my heart, mind, and soul.

Theodore Roosevelt said, "Nothing in the world is worth having or worth doing unless it means effort, pain, difficulty . . . I have never in my life envied a human being who led an easy life. I have envied a great many people who led difficult lives and led them well." In essence, anything worth having does not come easy. What could possibly be more worthy of having than our hearts, minds, and souls? Given this truth, then as Teddy stated, we need to make whatever effort and endure whatever pain/difficulties we encounter to ensure we protect them.

Working hard means the protection of our hearts, minds, and souls does not come easily. This hard work requires intentional living, daily attention to the process, and it also involves endurance. This protection is not a step or goal that is quantifiably achieved at a set point. It is an ongoing process that does not end until our last breath leaves our body. Hence, the need for endurance.

I write this book to protect my mind. I feed my mind with good things with every page I write. Personally, I know when I stop feeding my mind like this, too much garbage enters it. I protect my heart every day that I read my Bible, so it is important for me to read and pray on the words daily. Finally, I protect my soul by applying what I have read in Scripture to my day-to-day life.

Today, work hard, harder than ever, to safeguard, shield, insulate, defend, and care for your heart, mind, and soul. They are your greatest assets.

Rewrite the affirmation three times:

1. _____

2. _____

3. _____

Personal thoughts:

_____

_____

_____

_____

_____

_____

_____

_____

_____

Day 39

I do the job right the first time, so I do not have to do it again.

Though the saying "Time is money" might be too restrictive a definition of time, time *is* a very valuable asset. Because it is available in equal quantities to everybody, it is arguably also the most wasted asset.

For this reason, this affirmation takes on extreme importance. We need to respect time for its value and for how nonrenewable it is. By doing the job right the first time, we now have bankrolled future time to be allocated for something else, even rest and recreation. By not doing the job right the first time, we have saddled our future with debt—debt of having more to do in the future (this job again plus what was already planned) than time allows.

A side benefit of doing a job right the first time is it generates a reputation for excellence and dependability. This leads to advancement in your profession, respect of peers, increased wages, and a higher quality of people, above and below your pay grade, who wish to saddle up alongside you.

Another side benefit is reduced stress. Think about the last time you or someone else had to do a job over again. Deadlines are here or past, other things that you could be doing are now put on the back burner, and your life has now become more stressful than it needed to be.

Whether it is a work commitment or a weekend chore, take the time to do the job right the first time. Why burden your future unnecessarily?

Rewrite the affirmation three times:

1. _____

2. _____

3. _____

Personal thoughts:

_____

_____

_____

_____

_____

_____

_____

_____

_____

Day 40

I know what is important in my life.

What is important in your life is most likely ever-changing. The various stages in our lives yield different things that are important. From the little girl who without even realizing it knows the importance of her parents, to the college graduate looking for employment, to the couple nearing retirement, we all know what is important in our lives.

Sadly, knowing what is important and acting on what is important are two different things. Most of us do what is urgent in our lives versus what is important. In a 1954 speech, Dwight Eisenhower once said, "What is important is seldom urgent and what is urgent is seldom important." We internally recognize those things that are important to us, like relationships and health, but rarely do they carry a sense of urgency on a day-to-day basis, so we do not act on them. The urgent things are usually the result of external forces or people. Somebody needs something *now*. It is also on rare occasions that these urgent matters fall under *your* definition of what is important. They may be important to the one having the urgency, but rarely are they important for you.

On the blank lines opposite this page, take a few minutes to write down those things that are important to you and those things that are considered urgent. What will you do to pay some *intentional attention* to those matters that are important? We must find a way to do this on a regular basis because if we do not, those things that are important but not urgent will suddenly become important and extremely urgent.

Rewrite the affirmation three times:

1. _____

2. _____

3. _____

Personal thoughts:

_____

_____

_____

_____

_____

_____

_____

_____

_____

Day 41

I know the impact that service to others has on my joy.

In my youth, I often heard people say, "It is always better to give than to receive." Naturally I thought this was a bunch of garbage because more is always better, right? And if you give, you have less and not more. I also thought this was perhaps some con from someone who simply was trying to get more for themselves at my expense. What a fool I was!

It wasn't until my bouts with depression that I figured out the best way for me to get out of that state, and more importantly to stay out of that state, is to be of service to others. It provides me great joy to think this book may help someone, anyone. If someone takes to heart each of these affirmations, reinforces them by writing them out on the lines below, and then meditates on their personal meaning, they will be more joyful.

If you are going through a state of depression in your life, first and foremost, *please* seek medical attention. Secondly, even if you're not depressed but just not feeling good, look to be of service to someone else. The moment we look to be of service to someone else, our minds immediately shift away from our own situation. We move from the negative to the positive. Even before performing the act of service, you will have more joy in your life just by thinking about it.

Initially, the smile on your face as you serve others may seem artificial or false. However, the more you serve others, the quicker that smile will become genuine.

Rewrite the affirmation three times:

1. _____

2. _____

3. _____

Personal thoughts:

_____

_____

_____

_____

_____

_____

_____

_____

_____

_____

Day 42

I have a passion for success that is stronger than my fear of failure.

Time to get a little personal. I married when I was a senior in college. I didn't even tell my parents about the marriage until a couple of weeks later. Though we married for all the wrong reasons, the real reason our marriage failed after thirteen years is that I was a self-centered, self-absorbed idiot in my twenties.

I am sure I am not the only one who has ever experienced this. Many people, myself included at one point, have such a strong fear of failure after a marriage ends that they decide they will never marry again.

Eight years after my divorce, I met Teresa. After only two months of dating, we were married in a chapel on the Las Vegas strip. My parents met Teresa for the first time at the chapel, and even picked it out because Teresa and I were living in Virginia at the time. Immediately after meeting Teresa and deciding to get married, my passion to ensure a successful marriage became infinitely stronger than my fear of failure. Teresa, just by who she is, made me *want* to become a better person, a better husband, and a better father. Because I wanted to be better and was not being forced to be better, the passion for a successful marriage was ignited.

You cannot have a passion for success that is stronger than your fear of failure until you find something or someone you are passionate about. You cannot force the passion. It must happen organically for long-term success. Do not worry if your passion has not yet presented itself; it will someday. Keep your eyes open, keep your fear of failure in check, and soon you too will have this passion for success.

Rewrite the affirmation three times:

1. _____

2. _____

3. _____

Personal thoughts:

_____

_____

_____

_____

_____

_____

_____

_____

_____

_____

Day 43

I like the person I look at in the mirror.

S ometimes I look in the mirror and think, "Who is that old guy and how did he get in our house?" Because I don't like the appearance of the person in the mirror, I focus on the character and integrity of that person instead.

Every day, we are faced with decisions that, on the surface, seem individually innocuous but in the aggregate compile who we are as a person. Do we allow the person with their turn signal on to merge ahead of us or do we speed up? If we recognize after we have left the drive-thru that we were given too much change, do we turn around or drive away? How about the person at the corner holding the cardboard sign that says, "Homeless"? Do we help in any way? There are hundreds of instinctive decisions we make each day that help shape our character and integrity.

What about our mindset? Do we come across as happy-go-lucky even though we have angry or destructive thoughts racing inside our head? Our mindset is huge in determining our character and integrity because in crunch time we will default to what we predominantly think about.

The next time you look in the mirror, look past the physical façade (I am grateful to do that). Instead, look at the person beneath the skin veneer. Is it a person you would want your child to emulate? Or is it a person you would want them to avoid? Most likely, the person in the mirror is somewhere in-between. The great thing is you can change that person into whomever you want them to be.

Rewrite the affirmation three times:

1. _____

2. _____

3. _____

Personal thoughts:

_____

_____

_____

_____

_____

_____

_____

_____

_____

_____

Day 44

I am careful not to think or speak ill of others.

When I first wrote this affirmation, I did not have the word *think* in it. As I write this page, however, I am reminded that lately I have not been speaking ill of others, but I certainly have been thinking ill of them, hence the change. These people are understandably clueless about my thoughts. I have only been hurting myself.

More times than not, when we think ill of another, the only person we are actually hurting is ourself. When we constantly regurgitate reasons for thinking the way we do about another, right or wrong, it makes our lives miserable. The best thing to do in this situation is to recognize what we are doing to *ourselves* and then change the thought process. Some say we should actively think kind things about that other person, but let's get real . . . that isn't happening! But we can think of something else.

Even worse than thinking ill of someone is speaking ill of that person. This is worse for several reasons. First, when we speak ill of others, our character flaws stand out in the minds of the people to whom we are speaking. We become backstabbers. Secondly, when we hear our spoken words versus just thinking them, our thoughts are firmly embedded in our brains. Lastly, and most pragmatically, when we speak ill of others, nothing positive happens. The things that caused you to think/speak this way will only escalate.

Today, don't just nip ill speaking of others in the bud but avoid ill thoughts of others too. Why be the one to ruin your own day? Life may attempt to drag you down into the mud, but you do not have to assist it.

Rewrite the affirmation three times:

1. _____

2. _____

3. _____

Personal thoughts:

_____

_____

_____

_____

_____

_____

_____

_____

_____

_____

Day 45

I am rededicated to the priorities of my life.

O
ur lives are marathons. As with any kind of endurance race, there will be challenges. The biggest problem in the life race is that over time, we become so wrapped up in our day-to-day existence that we lose sight of the real priorities in our lives, and they go by the wayside. We are left with unfulfilling lives.

Do you know what your priorities in life are? Health? For most people, on January 1 this is their priority . . . until January 15 when . . . not so much. Is it your relationships? Career? Spirituality? What are your priorities? I guarantee that because we are different, we all have different, excellent priorities.

We must avoid getting wrapped up in day-to-day living at the expense of our personal priorities. We should regularly take time to reevaluate and rededicate ourselves to the priorities of our lives. For some, this may take place daily. For others, it may be weekly or perhaps monthly. Personally, I find that time spent weekly on my priorities is perfect. Evaluation more often tends to interfere with my day-to-day life, and any longer than a couple of weeks and I am trying to recapture ground I had gained previously but then lost recently.

How are we doing with the priorities we set in January? Is it time to rededicate ourselves to them? Should we have this rededication on a more frequent basis? Do we need to eliminate some priorities and create new ones? No matter how many months are left in this year, let's make it the best year ever! Rededicate yourself to your priorities!

Rewrite the affirmation three times:

1. _____

2. _____

3. _____

Personal thoughts:

_____

_____

_____

_____

_____

_____

_____

_____

_____

_____

Day 46

I work hard to grow new beans instead of counting old beans.

At first, many people will jump to the conclusion that this affirmation references money. I guess that is fair because that is what I was thinking when I first wrote it many years ago. Perhaps this is where the term *bean counter* originated. Motivational speaker Tony Robbins once shared that people will do more to keep someone from taking their money than they will to create new money. For the purpose of this affirmation, growing new beans instead of counting old beans means to create or grow something new in *any area of your life* instead of hanging on to something you already possess. At this stage of my life, my *beans* refer to *memories.*

So many of us hold on desperately to our memories, and some hang on at the risk of losing their future or even the present, for that matter. We often hear, "Remember when . . .?" Or "Back in my day . . ." Memories are a good thing, but we must work equally hard to create or grow new memories.

We must know that whatever our age, our financial position, or our health status, the present moment is just one season in our lives. The next decade or even the next year will be new seasons. What great memories are we going to create today?

For me, I will remember my past, but I will also create new memories today. What is your bean? What new bean will you work hard to grow today?

Rewrite the affirmation three times:

1. _____

2. _____

3. _____

Personal thoughts:

_____

_____

_____

_____

_____

_____

_____

_____

_____

_____

Day 47

I know present challenges are not life-and-death situations.

While we do indeed encounter some legitimate life-and-death situations, for the most part I think we would all agree that 99.9 percent of the challenges we face on a daily basis do not fall into this category. The sun is still going to rise from the east and set in the west, and a new day will begin again.

The problem with treating everyday challenges as life-and-death situations lies not in the challenge or the way we handle it; the problem is the needless, added stress we inflict upon ourselves for something not life or death.

We live in a world where many things are done in an instant. We are conditioned for immediacy. We get news from around the world the minute it is happening. Our meals are microwaved or come from a fast-food line and are eaten while driving. We have grown accustomed to not waiting for anything; challenges are no different. We want a challenge resolved now, and we want to move on to the next situation.

By treating present challenges like they are life and death, we tend to drag those closest to us into the situation. Not only have we created needless stress in our own life, but we have now heaped some more stress onto another's life as well. Stop it!

Acknowledge that present challenges are not life-and-death situations. As soon as we discover that these challenges will be resolved in the proper time, the happier our lives will become on a daily basis.

Rewrite the affirmation three times:

1. _____

2. _____

3. _____

Personal thoughts:

_____

_____

_____

_____

_____

_____

_____

_____

_____

_____

Day 48

I choose to make challenges blessings in disguise.

C ontinuing the theme of embracing life's challenges, you've probably heard the story about Michael Jordan getting cut from his high school basketball team and then going on to become arguably the greatest player ever. Being cut from his high school team could be considered a blessing in disguise because it forced him to work even harder to make the team. That challenge obviously paid off.

We all face challenges every day. When I was going through a period of depression, some of my biggest challenges were to simply get out of bed in the morning, shower, and get to work. What challenges are you facing right now?

The key to making challenges blessings in disguise is to be prepared in advance to transform them when they arise. If we wait until a challenge is upon us, more than likely we will be so wrapped up getting through the challenge that we will not even consider how we can use it to be a blessing. This might be one of those affirmations that you repeat to yourself every single day, not just once, but multiple times. By doing so, when a challenge presents itself, you will act on reflex to turn it into a blessing in disguise.

How we react to the challenges we face not only impacts us, but it also impacts those closest to us. We become role models on how to navigate through a challenge and how to use the challenge to our benefit.

How can you turn a challenge you are currently facing into a blessing?

Rewrite the affirmation three times:

1. _____

2. _____

3. _____

Personal thoughts:

_____

_____

_____

_____

_____

_____

_____

_____

_____

Day 49

I know the longer I carry a problem, the heavier it gets.

I once saw a war movie where prisoners of war were forced to have their arms extended from their sides while holding a bucket of water in each hand. If they let the bucket drop or touch the ground, they were beaten. There is also a Biblical story in Exodus 17:12–13 where if Moses held up his arms while overseeing a battle, the Israelites began winning the battle. As soon as his arms dropped, they would start to lose. So, Moses had two others help by holding his arms up. These are two classic examples, one from Hollywood and one from Scripture, showing that the longer we carry a problem, the heavier it gets.

For many of us, myself included at times, we procrastinate getting a problem resolved simply because we do not want to deal with it. This problem could be work related, health related, something that is broken at home, or it could even be with another person. The problem with procrastinating is that the problem persists over time and may have gotten worse. How many people diagnosed with cancer ever had their cancer completely go away simply by ignoring it? Usually, left untreated, the cancer gets worse/heavier.

Would you like the burdens you are currently experiencing to be removed from your life right now, or at least made lighter? Begin by naming one problem you are carrying that you wish to have removed from your life. Once you identify this problem, I urge you to act today to get it resolved. It is not going to go away by itself and will only get heavier over time. Like Moses, reach out for help if needed. Start today to lighten your load.

Rewrite the affirmation three times:

1. _____

2. _____

3. _____

Personal thoughts:

_____

_____

_____

_____

_____

_____

_____

_____

_____

_____

Day 50

I know the cost of my future is based on the price I pay today.

What is your vision for your future? What will it cost you in terms of the price you are willing to pay today? I know so many people whose futures are extraordinarily bright and an equal number of people whose futures are bleak because of how they live today. The difference between the two futures is not based on who they are or their talents, careers, or family. It is based on what they do or did in moments today and years ago.

For the people whose future is bright, they took care of business today in all facets of their lives. They worked today like nobody else so they could live like nobody else tomorrow. That meant living within one's means/budget. Also, instead of procrastinating about their health, they exercised and ate properly. In terms of their relationships, they treated their spouse every day like they were dating. Cumulatively, this is the price they were willing to pay today for their future.

The opposite can be said for those people whose futures will be hard. For whatever reason, they were not willing to pay the price on a given day to ensure a bright tomorrow. For some, they lived in constant debt. For others, they neglected their health and/or their relationships. They sacrificed their future for a few moments today that will be gone tomorrow.

You *must* know that it is never too late to make your future better. It does not matter if you are in your teens or senior years; you can still make tomorrow better. But you must be willing to pay the price—today. Are you willing?

Rewrite the affirmation three times:

1. _____

2. _____

3. _____

Personal thoughts:

_____

_____

_____

_____

_____

_____

_____

_____

_____

Day 51

I live my life in the manner I wish my children to live theirs.

As our children have children of their own, I try to impress upon them that their most important job from now until they die is to be a proper role model for their children. Our children watch and learn from us. They watch how we handle relationships with our spouses and with them. They watch our work ethic, how we maintain a household, our health, our spirituality; they watch everything.

Sadly, it was not until my children were fully grown that I realized this fact. Don't get me wrong, I was a good parent and my children will attest to that, but I could have been so much better if I had only grasped this concept early on.

Now that I am in my sixties and our children are in their thirties and having children of their own, I realize that I am still a role model for them, even if they live across the country or in the next town. They are watching how my bride and I navigate the transition into retirement. They watch how we work to maintain our health. They are watching to see if we are leading a Godly life or whether we just talk about it.

No matter our age, we must live our lives in a manner we wish our children to live theirs. This is *not* to say they must live *their* lives like we live ours. This affirmation is all about our being the best people and the best role models we can be, not only to our children, but to everyone around us. The world is watching.

I vow to live my life in the manner I wish my children to live theirs. Will you?

Rewrite the affirmation three times:

1. _____

2. _____

3. _____

Personal thoughts:

_____

_____

_____

_____

_____

_____

_____

_____

_____

_____

Day 52

I change today so tomorrow will be better than yesterday.

Looking back at my life, I am incredibly blessed. I also know that I have I have been given many talents that I wasted or did not fully use.

We all have three distinct time zones in our lives. The first is the Yesterday Time Zone (YTZ). In the YTZ, all the things we said and did in the past reside. The truth about the YTZ is that we cannot do a single thing to change it, at least until a time-travel machine is developed. Then we have the Tomorrow Time Zone (TTZ). While we cannot predict exactly what will happen tomorrow, we can help shape it so that it is at least better than the YTZ. How do we shape it? We shape the TTZ by what we do in the This Day Time Zone (TDTZ).

If we are honest with ourselves, there are two things I am confident we all can agree on. The first is that we can be a better person. The second is, no matter how great our lives are today, we would be thrilled if our tomorrow were better than yesterday.

Looking back at our YTZ, what things would you change if you had the opportunity? How would those changes have made today better? Now, look ahead to the TTZ. What changes can you make today in the TDTZ? How will that make tomorrow better than yesterday?

I know that if I want tomorrow to be better, I must be willing to change today.

Rewrite the affirmation three times:

1. _____

2. _____

3. _____

Personal thoughts:

_____

_____

_____

_____

_____

_____

_____

_____

_____

Day 53

I understand the power of vision plus intentional action.

Picture this scenario. You are all alone on a sailboat, you can clearly see the island you want to visit, and it is miles in the distance. A gentle wind is blowing. Now add to the picture a broken rudder and the realization that you have absolutely no way of steering your boat to the island. This is an example of having a vision but no intentional action.

Now picture another scenario. The wind is blowing, your boat is in tip-top condition, and you are smooth sailing. You are flying along the water, but you have no clue about where you are going. This is an example of having plenty of action but no vision of where you wish to go. You may end up in pirate territory.

These are simplistic scenarios, but our lives are run the same way. If we have a vision of where we want our lives to head but take no intentional action to get ourselves there, the chances of achieving our vision are slim to none. Conversely, if we are working ourselves to the bone but have no vision of where we want to end up, we will get someplace fast but won't know where that place will be.

After completing these months of exercises, I hope you understand the power of combining your vision with intentional action. Rest assured, without them working in tandem, you will wind up somewhere, but it just might not be where you want to end up.

Rewrite the affirmation three times:

1. _____

2. _____

3. _____

Personal thoughts:

_____

_____

_____

_____

_____

_____

_____

_____

_____

_____

Day 54

I am kind even if others would understand if I wasn't.

This affirmation goes much further than the old "eye for an eye, tooth for a tooth" mentality. That mindset is all about reciprocation and punishment. While appropriate in criminal and civil matters adjudicated in court, it should not apply to ordinary, day-to-day grievances we have with others.

With people, we should not only avoid the eye-for-an-eye mentality, but we should seek to be kind even if everyone would not fault us if we were not.

Being wronged can hurt us two ways. The first hurt is from whomever or whatever wronged us in the beginning. The second hurt we potentially do to ourselves. By plotting retaliatory actions or even thinking ugly thoughts, we hurt ourselves a second time by the negativity running rampant in our heads. We must rise above thinking even neutral thoughts to thinking thoughts of kindness toward whomever or whatever wronged us. Scientists have discovered that we change the chemical balances in our brains based on what we are thinking. The first hurt we experienced was more than enough; kindness will level the field.

This kindness toward another may even implant in them a better way to go about life. It might be the light bulb they need to make changes in their own life.

This will *not* be easy. It flies completely against human nature and will take massive work to accomplish. But if we are kind, even if the world would understand if we were not, we have instantly made our own lives better.

Rewrite the affirmation three times:

1. _____

2. _____

3. _____

Personal thoughts:

_____

_____

_____

_____

_____

_____

_____

_____

_____

Day 55

I judge each day by the seeds I plant and those I nurture.

This is like the old saying, "Whatever you feed grows and whatever you starve dies." We are speaking of the seeds in life that bear fruit. This applies to new seeds that you have an opportunity to plant today as well as seeds you have planted in the past and are now nurturing. Seeds include those planted in you and those you plant in the people around you.

Within yourself, what previously planted seeds need nurturing? What seeds still need to be planted? The reading and completion of the exercises in this book are a testament to the nurturing of the seeds you planted within yourself to become a better you. Congratulations! What other seeds in your life need nurturing? What new seed do you need to plant within yourself? This is the seed that you have been yearning to plant but have just not gotten around to yet. Could it be something educational? Spiritual? Health-oriented? What are you waiting for? Go plant!

What seeds that you've sown in those around you need nurturing? Could it be a child, friend, or spouse that needs a little TLC? How can you improve their lives today? It is foolish to have a seed that you once planted, and that was previously thriving, be neglected to the point where it dies. If this is the case, why did you plant it in the first place? What new seed can you plant in someone's life today?

Judge today both by the new seeds you planted in yourself and others and those previously planted seeds that you nurtured. How did you do?

Rewrite the affirmation three times:

1. _____

2. _____

3. _____

Personal thoughts:

_____

_____

_____

_____

_____

_____

_____

_____

_____

_____

Day 56

I anticipate problems and then address them before they arrive.

I am not saying that we should worry over problems that are not present or make up problems when there is a slim chance they will happen. More times than not, the things we worry about the most never come to fruition. This affirmation speaks to not being blindsided when typical, day-to-day problems materialize.

What types of problems can we anticipate? Instantly, I think of unexpected car problems, babysitters who cancel, sickness in us or others, home repairs, and the list goes on.

When we anticipate problems and address them before they arrive, essentially, we are talking about having a backup plan. In the aforementioned areas like car or home repairs, a backup plan involves having an emergency fund set aside specifically for these types of emergencies. A rule of thumb for an emergency fund is four to six months of household expenses. It is unrealistic to think that one will create a fully funded emergency account overnight. Start small, perhaps by working to have one month of household expenses in an account reserved for those types of emergencies. Other types of problems that do not involve money can certainly throw a monkey wrench into our lives. Work on a backup plan and then periodically put it into play. For example, secure a backup babysitter and use them occasionally to ensure they are still a viable option.

We should not go out of our way to plan for problems that may never exist. However, it is foolish not to anticipate and address daily issues that may arise.

Rewrite the affirmation three times:

1. _____

2. _____

3. _____

Personal thoughts:

_____

_____

_____

_____

_____

_____

_____

_____

_____

_____

Day 57

I transform great ideas into great action.

Do you know what is great about a great idea? Absolutely nothing! Everybody has some sort of an idea, and what is to say that it is great? Great ideas are a dime a dozen. In fact, there are literally thousands of people who probably had the same idea. That is what makes ideas so cheap. They are worthless until action is taken to turn them from an idea into reality.

Here is where the best part of this affirmation lies. Most people think a great idea is something global that will save mankind. But the reality is that you can have a great idea that only involves you and your own little world. How cool is that? So right now, let's get out of the mindset that a great idea must be globally monumental for it to be great. Your great idea can be exclusively for a party of one . . . you. But we still must act, or it remains worthless. Before moving forward with acting on your great idea, however, ask yourself this important question: Is my great idea worth the time, effort, and possible financial investment that may be required?

If you conclude that it is, the first action step to take is to flesh out the great idea. We cannot be so arrogant to think that this great idea is an original idea, or that there is no one that can make the idea even greater. With that in mind, research the idea to find out why the idea has or has not worked for others. People to contact could be friends, relatives, mentors, or even online experts.

You indeed have great ideas, so don't kill them off by failing to act.

Rewrite the affirmation three times:

1. _____

2. _____

3. _____

Personal thoughts:

_____

_____

_____

_____

_____

_____

_____

_____

_____

_____

Day 58

I realize fences shut me in while keeping others out.

Back in the early 1970s, one of my favorite songs was "Signs" by the Five Man Electrical Band. The song was principally about signs meant to exclude people. I remember one lyric of the song fifty years later as I write this affirmation. The lyric was about a sign on a fence and the singer questioned the need for the fence. Was it to keep people out, or imprison things inside?

Physical fences come in many forms, seen and unseen. But I think perhaps the most beneficial and, at the same time, potentially destructive types of fences we install are the emotional fences we put around our own lives. As the affirmation states, while most emotional fences are designed to keep others out, they also shut us in. We cannot have one effect without the other.

Sometimes we need to put up an emotional fence to keep the pain of a toxic relationship or situation at bay. It is self-preservation for our mind. Without this fence, we may very well go down the rabbit hole of despair and depression.

However, while this fence protects our mental health, we must also realize it has an adverse effect on our personal growth. To grow as people, we must be able to properly work with and through all types of people and situations.

Emotional fences have a time and place for proper use. We must be wise enough to know when to erect them and when to take them down. What fences have you built around yourself? Is it time to take any of them down and grow?

Rewrite the affirmation three times:

1. _____

2. _____

3. _____

Personal thoughts:

_____

_____

_____

_____

_____

_____

_____

_____

_____

Day 59

To get what I need, I must first help someone get what they need.

F amous motivation speaker Zig Ziglar once stated, "You can have everything in life that you want, if you will just help other people get what they want." Another spin on this idea came from Brian Lytle, one of the finest real estate attorneys in the country. One of the best classes he ever taught was called The Art of Negotiations. Mr. Lytle taught that if you want your home buyer client to get what they need out of the transaction, seek first to help the seller get what they need, if it does not negatively impact your buyer client.

It has become so clear to me that if I need something, and it does not seem to be materializing, I should seek out someone who is in need themselves and help however I can. Amazingly, when I do this, either what I need comes to fruition 100 percent of the time, or it becomes clear that I really didn't need it after all. Some people might call this karma, while others say, "What goes around comes around" (though this is usually spoken of in terms of paying back evil for evil).

An extremely important facet about helping someone else get what they want is your motivation to help them. We shouldn't be seeking to help someone just for what we will possibly get out of it. We must genuinely seek to help someone regardless of the rewards or result. Your heart matters!

If you find yourself in need, seek to help someone get what they need with no ulterior motive. You will be surprised at how your life will be transformed and will lack for nothing.

Rewrite the affirmation three times:

1. _____

2. _____

3. _____

Personal thoughts:

_____

_____

_____

_____

_____

_____

_____

_____

_____

_____

Day 60

I have eliminated the emotional debris from my head.

Waste, *refuse, rubbish, ruins, wreckage, junk, rubble, trash,* and *garbage.* Those are all synonyms for *debris.* I can certainly store a bunch of that stuff in my head.

What kind of emotional debris do we carry around in our heads? Most likely, this debris manifests itself in the form of anger, unforgiveness, or vengeance, to name a few. I remember one time when I was driving and entering a merge area. A driver who was far behind me in the next lane sped up just to cut in front of me at the last second. I had to swerve onto the shoulder to avoid them. I sounded my horn in anger but resisted flipping the bird. However, what I did not resist was the anger, that emotional debris, and it stayed in my head for the remainder of the day. I allowed this emotional debris to ruin my day and to affect those around me.

Removing the emotional debris from our heads is not that difficult. It involves merely changing what our minds focus on. What is difficult is keeping the debris from coming back. Once removed, if we do not replace it with something positive (not different emotional debris), it will come back, and when it does, it comes back with vengeance. We *must* change our mindset and keep it changed, not just leave it in a neutral position.

When emotional debris starts to junk up your head, exchange that debris for emotional thoughts of order, neatness, and cleanliness (all debris antonyms). Why do we insist on keeping this debris in our lives when it serves absolutely no purpose? Today is the time for a little spring cleaning of our emotional debris.

Rewrite the affirmation three times:

1. _____

2. _____

3. _____

Personal thoughts:

_____

_____

_____

_____

_____

_____

_____

_____

_____

_____

Day 61

I approach each task as if my legacy depends on it.

What do you want written on your tombstone? How would you like to be remembered when you are eulogized at your funeral, and how will people remember you in the years after you pass? This is your legacy.

The point of this affirmation is not to say that with everything you do, do it like your life depends on it. That is impossible and exhausting at the very least. What it does mean, however, is to approach every task with thanksgiving and a sincere desire to be of service to mankind. It means not begrudging what is ours to do.

This does not just apply to tasks that are grandiose. It means even the mundane tasks. For example, our household chores. Instead of bemoaning the fact that we would rather be doing anything other than cutting the grass on a beautiful Saturday morning, we can be thankful that we have a home with grass to cut.

When our employer or even our pastor asks us to take on a project, instead of accepting and then going home to complain about it to anyone who will listen, we should embrace the task and give it our best effort. Think about it—we can now be of service to someone who genuinely needs and appreciates our skill set.

The magnitude and the quality of the task to be completed is not nearly as important as the attitude with which we take on and complete the task. *That* is our legacy. Let us start creating the legacy we desire . . . today!

Rewrite the affirmation three times:

1. _____

2. _____

3. _____

Personal thoughts:

_____

_____

_____

_____

_____

_____

_____

_____

_____

Day 62

I strive for what is just beyond my grasp.

Sadly, many people live their lives with what I refer to as "T. rex arms." They are short, bent at the elbow, and never fully reach out for anything. For us to live full and meaningful lives, we must figuratively reach for our desires, even if at the present time they are just beyond our grasp.

Probably the two biggest areas to illustrate this affirmation include fitness and finances. In fitness, most people do not start out bench pressing 225 pounds or by running a six-minute mile. However, if that is their goal, they create programs and routines that constantly push themselves to achieve mini goals that are just beyond their reach. Over time, aka *perseverance*, they will reach their ultimate goals.

It is the same with our finances and material possessions. Most of us do not have lots of money in the bank when we enter adulthood. Through perseverance and planning, we can gradually increase our bank balance until it reaches our ultimate goal. Same principle with our possessions. I have never seen anybody buy a mansion on the water for their first home. Instead, it is usually a modest home they later sell to make a profit that they invest in their next home, a process they repeat until they are living in their dream home.

Together, let us strive for our goals in life by shedding our T. rex arms. When we use our abilities, plans, and perseverance to continually shoot for what is just beyond our reach, that which is way out of our reach is suddenly right before us.

Rewrite the affirmation three times:

1. _____

2. _____

3. _____

Personal thoughts:

_____

_____

_____

_____

_____

_____

_____

_____

_____

_____

_____

Day 63

I wholeheartedly give myself to this day.

O kay, a few scenarios for you to ponder on. If you were being tried in a court of law for a crime you did not commit, would you want your attorney to represent you wholeheartedly or half-heartedly? If you are married, would you want your spouse to love you wholeheartedly or half-heartedly? Of course, these answers are obvious. We gain so much more when things are done wholeheartedly.

The same principle applies to how we conduct our day. Why should we expect the results we desire if we are not willing to put in the effort required? You are thinking that it is impossible to give yourself wholeheartedly 100 percent of the time and you are correct. But think of the results your life will have in terms of achievement and satisfaction if you give wholeheartedly of yourself 75 percent, 50 percent, or even 25 percent of the day instead of half-heartedly 100 percent of the time?

Please keep in mind that giving of yourself wholeheartedly not only applies to work but also to play and rest. If you are taking the time to play, forget about work and . . . *play*! The enjoyment you will receive from that playtime will carry over into the work part of your life, making even your work more enjoyable. And if it is time to rest, then, you guessed it . . . *rest* wholeheartedly. Disconnect from technology, work, obligations, etc. Resting wholeheartedly is critical to every facet of your life.

Right now, pick an activity or even a time period, and give yourself wholeheartedly to it. Then see how you feel afterward.

Rewrite the affirmation three times:

1. _____

2. _____

3. _____

Personal thoughts:

_____

_____

_____

_____

_____

_____

_____

_____

_____

_____

Day 64

I survive both adversity and prosperity.

The word *survive* often refers to overcoming something negative. I survived being robbed, a bad car wreck, a heart attack, a tornado, or an abusive relationship. Those are all very adverse circumstances and can be deadly.

Why do we not think about surviving prosperity? Let's be clear: although most people measure prosperity in financial terms, even poor people may consider themselves prosperous. Prosperity is ultimately defined by the individual. For this affirmation, however, let's use the most common definition of prosperity and focus on the financial aspect.

For most people, financial prosperity is considered good, a positive, something to be desired. However, have you ever known someone or heard of someone who let prosperity go to their head? When this happens, people let prosperity affect how they live by making bad choices. We often see them trying to live the lives of celebrities on TV. For example, making expensive purchases/trips and foolish investments, choosing unhealthy eating/drinking, and so on. Before they know it, they realize what many others before them have experienced: prosperity can be fleeting and leave you worse than before.

Surviving prosperity is different from surviving adversity. When you survive adversity, it typically is not caused by you, yet you experience it. When it comes to prosperity, you do not have to just survive in it, you can *thrive* in it. The best and surest way to survive prosperity is to first recognize that the definition of financial prosperity is not the same for everybody. If you are feeling prosperous, enjoy it, and then make plans to safeguard your personal prosperity by making wise choices.

Rewrite the affirmation three times:

1. _____

2. _____

3. _____

Personal thoughts:

_____

_____

_____

_____

_____

_____

_____

_____

_____

Day 65

I work hard even when I do not want to.

Early in my real estate career, I started following a national trainer for real estate agents. His name is Mike Ferry (to this day he probably doesn't know who I am). Being fresh out of my first career as an officer in the United States Air Force, I was used to following orders, particularly in any endeavor I knew little about. I remember in one of Mr. Ferry's seminars, he said, "If I spent the day right alongside you, would you work any different than you do in any other day?" Needless to say, you know what everyone thought: "Of course!" We seem to work harder when we are facing a deadline of some sort or when someone is watching.

Face it, none of us want to work hard every day. In fact, I would guess that there are very few days when we want to work hard. Life is full of distractions to keep us from working hard, and if these distractions do not materialize on their own, we often conjure them up ourselves.

However, it is on those days, if we work hard when we do not want to, that we grow and start to achieve. This principle applies to every facet of life. Our greatest strides forward in physical fitness happen when we work hard on days we do not want to. Our greatest strides in our relationships happen when we work hard at them, even when we do not want to. Working hard when we do not feel like it affects our job performance and even our volunteer efforts.

The next time you do not want to work hard at something, remember this affirmation and push forward with all your strength. Then see how you feel.

Rewrite the affirmation three times:

1. _____

2. _____

3. _____

Personal thoughts:

_____

_____

_____

_____

_____

_____

_____

_____

_____

_____

Day 66

I avoid having irritations ruin my day.

R eading this affirmation, I am tempted to move it to Day 1 and then repeat it for the remaining ninety-nine days. As humans we have so much good going on in our lives, and yet we seem to focus on the irritations of the day. Note, I said *irritations*, not *problems*. We could have hundreds of five-star ratings from clients, but we will focus on the one client who seems to be terminally unhappy with us and with life. Or perhaps we could be dwelling on the dysfunctional family member instead of all the other relatives who bring joy into our lives.

Personally, when I am very busy, it is easy to avoid contemplating these irritants. However, when I am not so busy, or if I am doing something routine that doesn't require concentrated thought (like cutting the grass or driving a great distance on the interstate), I do tend to focus on these irritants.

Fortunately, I now recognize the times when I dwell on irritants. Because I recognize these moments, I can plan for them. It might sound weird (in fact, it *is* weird), but I plan what I am going to think about when I am cutting the grass. I plan what I am going to think about during that one-hour drive down the interstate. This allows me to control my thoughts and avoid having those irritants ruin my day.

Today, take notice of the irritants in your life and, more importantly, identify when they seem to occupy your mindset. Then *plan* to dwell on something more uplifting.

Rewrite the affirmation three times:

1. _____

2. _____

3. _____

Personal thoughts:

_____

_____

_____

_____

_____

_____

_____

_____

_____

_____

Day 67

I persevere long after the others have quit.

We have all heard the stories about the tortoise and the hare, Alexander Graham Bell's telephone, and any scientist who has ever made a significant discovery. Perseverance seems to be the well-known secret to success. I doubt we could find even one person who would claim that perseverance is a bad thing.

If everybody agrees that perseverance is a good thing, why do so few people persevere? I believe it is because we live in a fast-food mentality world. We want it all and we want it now. From our dinners to our financial security, we want it now. God forbid a teenager not getting their own car when they turn sixteen. Or, equally appalling, an adult child having to wait until they are older to have the same standard of living as their parents who have worked full-time jobs for forty years. The consequence of this thinking is massive, almost insurmountable debt.

It seems like perseverance is no longer seen as desirable, but rather as a punishment. Instead of the light at the end of the tunnel, all people see is the long, dark tunnel. To shake this mindset, it helps to first look at people who have taken shortcuts and see where they are in life. In most cases, it's not a desirable outcome. Secondly, we need to shift our focus onto the long-term goal itself and what that will mean to us instead of the length of time it will take to achieve that goal. To you reading this affirmation, take it from someone in the latter quarter of life—time indeed goes by quickly; it will not take as long as it seems.

Today, whatever it is for you, make it a point that you *will* persevere.

Rewrite the affirmation three times:

1. _____

2. _____

3. _____

Personal thoughts:

_____

_____

_____

_____

_____

_____

_____

_____

_____

_____

Day 68

I am fully engaged with the people I am with.

Have you ever been around someone who is looking at their phone, their watch, or around the room while you are speaking directly with them? Constantly responding with "uh-huh" and the like? How does that make you feel? Do we want others feeling the same way when they are engaged with us?

Outside of being loved, perhaps the biggest need we have is to feel wanted, respected, and validated. The best way for us to do this is to truly engage one-on-one with another person. When we are engaged with another, there are two things we can specifically do to make that person feel wanted, respected, and validated. The first is to look them in the eye. This does not mean that you are having a stare down with them—that is creepy. It means that you look at them a comfortable amount of time and you avoid looking at other things.

The second way is to periodically repeat and affirm what they are saying to ensure you understand what they are talking about. Again, this is not about reciting back to them word for word what they have said because that too is creepy. It means to periodically affirm you heard what they said by summarizing, in little snippets, what they told you.

The next time you are engaged in a conversation, be fully present and engaged in that moment. Take the time to look them in the eye, and take the time to repeat back to them what you heard. I promise, both you and they will feel good.

Rewrite the affirmation three times:

1. _____

2. _____

3. _____

Personal thoughts:

_____

_____

_____

_____

_____

_____

_____

_____

_____

_____

Day 69

I succeed because I am willing to succeed.

Let's be clear. One person's definition of succeeding may be, and often is, very different from another's. For one, they may measure success by how much money they earn or how many material goods they have accumulated. It is the adage, "He who dies with the most stuff, wins." For another, they may measure their success not by things of this earth, but in regards to their position in eternity.

Whatever your definition of success, you must first be willing to succeed. Sounds kind of ridiculous to not be willing to succeed, doesn't it? Believe it or not, many people are not willing to succeed. Why not?

For some, success requires work and, once again, that may be considered a four-letter word. They simply are not willing to put the work into succeeding. For others, it means they may have to change something in their personal habits. For example, it may require them to change their spending habits, sleeping habits, or how they interact with others. For someone who equates success with where they will spend eternity, it may involve completely changing who they are, what they do, and how they think. This can be very daunting.

Are you willing to succeed? Ask yourself these three questions: First, what is your personal definition of success? (This is huge and the cornerstone of this affirmation.) Second, what must happen for you to experience your personal success? Third, are you willing to put in the work, yes *work*, for this success? Take time now to record your answers.

Rewrite the affirmation three times:

1. _____

2. _____

3. _____

Personal thoughts:

_____

_____

_____

_____

_____

_____

_____

_____

_____

Day 70

I get my greatest joy when I serve others.

Have you ever come to the aid of a good friend? How about a total stranger? How did it make you feel? Humans have a built-in need to be of service to others. If you don't believe me, look at all the charitable organizations in your immediate area. There are organizations that feed people, shelter people, provide employment for people, and the list goes on. They were all started by someone with a need to serve and then staffed by more people, usually volunteers, with a need to serve.

There is a flip side to this need to serve, and that is needing to be served (helped) ourselves. I don't know about you, but whenever I need help, it makes me feel horrible. My thought process usually goes something like this: "They have too much on their plate already, they do not need to be helping me." It was not until recently that someone pointed out to me this very affirmation about great joy when serving others. This feeling is not limited to self-centered me. Everyone has great joy in serving others. When I deny someone the opportunity to serve/help me, I am depriving that person of an opportunity to experience great joy. I *must* get my ego in check and allow others to help me when I need help.

Most days, we all have the same routine of getting up, going to work, going home, and repeating it all the next day. This routine can destroy a person's joy. Today, if you feel joy lacking in your life, look for someone or some organization to serve, even one time. Also, if you need help, please do not allow your ego to prevent someone else from receiving great joy by being of service to you.

Rewrite the affirmation three times:

1. _____

2. _____

3. _____

Personal thoughts:

_____

_____

_____

_____

_____

_____

_____

_____

_____

Day 71

I seek to be a moment of joy in the lives of others.

In full transparency, a main reason I seek to be a moment of joy in the lives of others is for purely selfish motives. I personally take joy in that moment and for a long time afterward. Finding some bad dad joke and then relaying that to someone, knowing they can't help but roll their eyes and laugh, is like mainlining sugar. Or pulling an innocent prank on someone, knowing that deep inside they take joy in the fact you spent time thinking to do this to them, is priceless.

When you seek to be a moment of joy to another, you provide yourself with joy for an even longer period. Why? You now have a memory that when recalled brings still more joy back to you. When you spend time thinking about this moment of joy for another, even if it's only thirty seconds, it brings that joy back to you ten-fold.

A moment of joy you bring to the lives of others does not have to be elaborate, orchestrated, or expensive. It could be a spontaneous, random act of kindness. For example, stopping to help when you see someone struggling to load their car with groceries. Or making a quick phone call in between appointments just to let someone know you care about them and were thinking of them. I promise that the few minutes you spend prior to that call, and the few minutes after that call, will generate joy for you that lasts and lasts.

Think of how you can be a moment of joy to the next person you meet. Maybe it is with just a smile or a compliment. You know how they feel; how do you feel?

Rewrite the affirmation three times:

1. _____

2. _____

3. _____

Personal thoughts:

_____

_____

_____

_____

_____

_____

_____

_____

_____

Day 72

I strive to be who I want my children to be.

Wow! Of all the affirmations I have written over the years, this one is an absolute favorite. Every time I read it, I am still stunned by its message. We all want the best for our children, and we want them to have better lives than we do and to be better people than we are. If this is not your wish, turn in your parent card right now.

Here is the million-dollar question: If we want our children to have better lives than ours, to be better people than we are, to enjoy the best that life has to offer, why do we not pursue those things for ourselves? What is stopping us from becoming who we want our children to be?

Let's be clear. Who we want our children to be is not the same as what we want them to have. Yes, we want our children to have healthy relationships, quality possessions, etc. But more importantly, we want them to be quality people. We want them to be respected not for what they have, but for who they are. We want them to embrace the world out of love and optimism instead of hate and pessimism. Guess what? Our children learn from us at every age, theirs and ours. They constantly witness who we are as people and how we navigate the waters of life. Face it! We are their examples.

Today, I am going to focus on being a kind, loving person who seeks to put the needs of others before my own. I want my children to say they are proud of me and want to grow up to be like me. If I strive to be who I want my children to be, then I must first show them the way. How about you?

Rewrite the affirmation three times:

1. _____

2. _____

3. _____

Personal thoughts:

_____

_____

_____

_____

_____

_____

_____

_____

_____

_____

Day 73

I avoid reliving the negativity of my past.

The first version of this affirmation had the word *recalling* in it as well. The more I thought about it though, the more I think it is okay to recall the negativity of your past because it can help you in the present or the future; we just shouldn't relive it. Have you ever seen the movie *Groundhog Day*? The main character relives the same day, Groundhog Day, every day. Nothing ever changes. This is what can happen to us when we continually relive the negativity of our past. We simply cannot grow, unless we choose to use that past experience for personal growth.

I used to be a victim of this habit. Not only would I recall a particular argument between my parents, mistreatment by a teacher, or something pertaining to a relationship I was in, I would relive it. *Why?* I bet the other participants in whatever I was reliving were not doing the same. Reliving that negativity of the past only hurt one person—me!

This is where a shift in mindset comes in. When I recall the negativity of my past, instead of reliving it, I choose to do one of two things. Either I will sincerely say a silent thank you for seeing how it changed my life for the better, or I will pretend this experience was happening to someone other than myself and think about how I would counsel them through that experience. By choosing this path of thinking, I do not relive it but benefit from it.

When you recall something negative from your past, embrace it but do not relive it. Instead, say a word of thanks that you survived it and became a better person because of it or, better yet, counsel yourself on how to make the most of it.

Rewrite the affirmation three times:

1. _____

2. _____

3. _____

Personal thoughts:

_____

_____

_____

_____

_____

_____

_____

_____

_____

Day 74

I have taken charge of my life.

Y ou are either in charge of your life, or someone or something else is. In the military, there is the commander and there are those who report to her. In the civilian sector, there is the employer and the employee. Somebody runs the show. The question for you right now is, who or what oversees your life?

What is in control of our lives, in charge if you will, are our habits. For the drug addict, alcoholic, workaholic, or couch potato, those things direct that person's life. The good news is that we can decide the habits we wish to have in our lives that will put us in charge. We might need help to overcome less productive habits but by doing so, we reaffirm that we indeed direct our lives.

Get out a pad of paper and draw a line dividing the paper in half. On one half, write down all the bad habits you have. They don't have to be huge. They could include being habitually late or having a rebellious, argumentative spirit. They could also include something as simple as hitting the snooze button multiple times. On the other half of the paper, write down your good habits. You know you have them. It doesn't matter what they are. If you do it habitually and it is a good thing, write it down.

Next, come up with a plan to eliminate one of the bad habits and a plan to reinforce one of the good habits. Again, it doesn't matter what it is, large or small, needing assistance or not. Write it down and then work on it. By doing so, you have taken charge of your life. Congratulations!

Rewrite the affirmation three times:

1. _____

2. _____

3. _____

Personal thoughts:

_____

_____

_____

_____

_____

_____

_____

_____

_____

_____

Day 75

I have let go of unrealistic expectations and their stress.

Initially, this affirmation focused primarily on unrealistic expectations I have for *myself*. As I started to think more about this, however, it hit me that sometimes I have unrealistic expectations of *others*, leading to stress for both me *and* them.

The unrealistic expectations of myself typically revolve around goal setting. They could be goals concerning my health, finances, personal growth, you name it. If I could create a goal, I could create an equally unrealistic expectation for myself. I would love to know what my blood pressure is during these times. Sadly, even with knowledge to the contrary, I still have the same tendencies today. For example, I think it is perfectly realistic for me to go to college full-time online plus work forty–sixty hours per week, all while leading a "balanced" life. Thank God I have Teresa in my life to help me manage my expectations.

But it gets worse. At times I will create unrealistic expectations for people around me. I think, *Come on! All it takes is self-discipline!* Though completely obvious to even the most casual observer, no two people are alike and that is a good thing. The world needs diversity. For me to place unrealistic expectations on others simply is not fair to them or me.

Honestly look at the expectations you have for yourself and those around you. If you cannot do this objectively, find your own Teresa and get someone to help you. Then manage those expectations so they are realistic and get rid of some stress. Life is meant to be enjoyed, not to be lived in self-induced stress.

Rewrite the affirmation three times:

1. _____

2. _____

3. _____

Personal thoughts:

_____

_____

_____

_____

_____

_____

_____

_____

_____

Day 76

I use my experience as a guidepost instead of a hitching post.

A guidepost is something that gives us guidance. It points us in the ways we wish to go or not go. Experience is our guidepost in life. A child who puts his hand on a hot stove is not likely to put his hand on a stove ever again unless he is certain it is cool. Likewise, an adult who gets caught speeding in an area notorious for being a speed trap is not likely to speed when driving in that area again. Experience can be used to guide us or act as a sign for future choices.

So, what do I mean by *hitching post*? Boy, that is an old term you don't hear much today, unless you're a fan of old western movies. A hitching post is something immovable that cowboys used to tie their horses to so the animal couldn't run off while the cowboy was gone. In this affirmation, we are using it symbolically to mean something that, based on your past experiences, keeps *you* in place, unable to move forward.

Our experiences in life are going to do one of two things for us. First, we are either going to learn from them, good or bad, and use that knowledge to move us forward in life, or two, they are going to tie us to the place we currently are. The world is moving forward, with or without us. If we are using hitching posts, not only are we not moving forward, but we are also moving backward as the world passes us by.

Think of two past experiences, one that has served to guide you forward in life and the other that you are using as an excuse, a hitching post, not to move forward. How can you unhitch yourself from the post that is holding you back?

Rewrite the affirmation three times:

1. _____

2. _____

3. _____

Personal thoughts:

_____

_____

_____

_____

_____

_____

_____

_____

_____

_____

Day 77

I recognize every moment is a precious gift.

R ecently we had a mini family reunion. For the first time ever, we had our four adult children and five grandchildren together. They came to visit from all parts of our country. It is times like these that make life so special. As the saying goes, "No one is promised tomorrow." In that context, it is easy to recognize every moment is a precious gift.

If that's true, why do we have to recognize only special occasions as precious moments? Why don't we recognize our day-to-day moments as precious gifts too? After all, time is still time, right?

As I reflect on this affirmation, a big *aha!* is clicking in my brain. How much more fulfilling would my life be if I took every moment, even the routine moments of every day, and considered them precious? Would my attitude change? Would I treat those around me any differently? I think the answer is a resounding *yes!*

Every moment is precious, not just those on special occasions. When we start treating our everyday life like it is a special occasion, because it indeed is, our lives will be changed forever. Driving down the road and seeing the blue sky and white clouds will bring a new appreciation. The conversations and interactions we have with others will have new meaning. I challenge you for the next five minutes to treat those five minutes as if they were the most precious minutes of your life. Cherish them. How does this make you feel? Go on, do it!

Rewrite the affirmation three times:

1. _____

2. _____

3. _____

Personal thoughts:

_____

_____

_____

_____

_____

_____

_____

_____

_____

_____

Day 78

I embrace rejection as it is a growth opportunity.

Nobody likes rejection, but there are some who embrace it. Many people never achieve what they desire for their lives because they fear even the thought of rejection. Others achieve their goals and dreams because they embrace rejection and use it as a learning tool. Which one are you?

Rejection can be a humbling experience. It can be seen not only as a failure, but a failure specifically directed at us. It has the possibility of indicating to ourselves and others that we simply are not good enough. This is such a horrible way to look at rejection. Instead, we should look to learn how rejection can enhance the chances of success next time. Rejection can be seen as a victory.

In real estate, we frequently make listing presentations where we explain to a home seller what we will do to get their home sold. Most times, a savvy home seller will interview several agents. No matter how good you are, there will be times when a seller chooses another agent to market their home—rejection. We make it a point to find out why we were not chosen. Sometimes, it was for reasons out of our control. For the other times, we reevaluated and made changes to our presentation that enhance our chances for success the next time.

Like most things, rejection is nothing more than a mindset. There is no one who has never been rejected. If you are breathing and trying to live a quality life, you have been and will be rejected. How we deal with rejection determines how far we go in life. Learn and grow from rejection. Embrace it!

Rewrite the affirmation three times:

1. _____

2. _____

3. _____

Personal thoughts:

_____

_____

_____

_____

_____

_____

_____

_____

_____

_____

Day 79

I polish my marriage daily.

If you are not married, please substitute your most important relationship for this affirmation. For those of us with children, we know that someday they will grow up and go out on their own. One day you will stop working. Friendships change. Even the churches and organizations we attend change. The one thing that should never change, except to get better, is your most important relationship here on earth. It is for this reason I choose to polish my relationship with my bride daily.

I know that everything in life, from bank accounts to health and so on, is fluid. I also know that it is very difficult to go through the roller coaster of life alone. We all need a partner with whom to experience the highs in life and to help us through the lows. My bride is with me every step of life's roller-coaster ride.

I polish my relationship with my bride by doing my best to be for her what I need her to be for me. When she needs a shoulder to lean on or a listening ear, I willingly pause whatever I am doing and provide that to her. And yes, sometimes it really is just an ear to hear her—she is not asking me to fix anything.

Think of that personal relationship you are in right now. What do they need from you? Are you providing it? We have mentioned before the need to have activities in our daily calendar that support our goals. Do you have activities in your daily calendar that support your most important earthly relationship? If not, incorporate some today and begin to polish that relationship. No matter how tarnished it is, it can always be shined up to its original brilliance.

Rewrite the affirmation three times:

1. _____

2. _____

3. _____

Personal thoughts:

_____

_____

_____

_____

_____

_____

_____

_____

_____

Day 80

I can't do everything, but I can do something.

Take a good look at the next airplane you see flying overhead. Now ask yourself: Did one person possess the technology and the materials to build that plane? Does a person building the plane even know how to fly it? Please inform me if you know one person who possesses the mind of Einstein, the compassion of Mother Teresa, the artistic talents of Michelangelo, and the athletic ability of Michael Jordan.

There is the saying, "It takes a village to raise a child." The same principle applies to life in general. As alluded to in the previous paragraph, nobody can do everything. However, as I've mentioned in several other contexts, everybody can do something. How do we know what this "something" is?

First, we must do a little self-evaluation. What do we know we can do? What do we know we cannot do? One person might be a good planner but a lousy executioner of plans. Still another might have plenty of money but zero time, while still another has lots of time but zero money. We all have something to contribute.

Once we know what we do and do not have, the next step is to look at the world around us. Who or what could use the resources you have, trusting that someone else will provide the resources you do not possess? Trust me, if you cannot find someone or something that you could help, simply tell another person about the available resources you have and see what happens next.

We can't do everything, but we can do something. What one small thing will you do that will make a difference today?

Rewrite the affirmation three times:

1. _____

2. _____

3. _____

Personal thoughts:

_____

_____

_____

_____

_____

_____

_____

_____

_____

_____

Day 81

I live life with an attitude of gratitude.

Daily, we live life with an attitude. For some it could be anger or happiness. For me, I choose to go through my life with an attitude of gratitude.

For Christmas one year, our boss gave each of us a book called *The Gratitude Journal*. Daily, we had to write down three things that we were most grateful for on that day. Honestly, some days I was grateful that the end of the book was drawing near. On other days, I could write down thirty things I was grateful for.

When we choose to live a life of gratitude, our mindset changes, even for just that moment in time. Can you think of a time in your life when you were incredibly grateful for something and yet very sad at the same time? Perhaps it was the death of a loved one after a lengthy battle with health issues. We are grateful they are no longer suffering but sad they have passed away.

Let's also keep in mind what an attitude is. It is not a momentary feeling. It is how we conduct ourselves and navigate through daily life, our modus operandi, if you will.

Today, intentionally live life with an attitude of gratitude. At the end of the day, ask yourself how it went. Did you find yourself less frustrated and smiling more? Then do it again tomorrow and the day after. After a while, you will be living your life in a perpetual attitude of gratitude.

Rewrite the affirmation three times:

1. _____

2. _____

3. _____

Personal thoughts:

_____

_____

_____

_____

_____

_____

_____

_____

_____

_____

Day 82

I know the difference between good and great is a little effort.

This affirmation seems to be at odds with the affirmation of Day 2, which reads, "I am at peace with imperfection." We explained this as follows: "If you find yourself in a situation where something is great but you believe it can be better, take a step back and objectively look at the situation. What is a better use of your time and energies: getting something perfect (if that's even possible), getting another project started, or perhaps just taking time to relax and breathe?"

Being at peace with imperfection runs along the lines of the law of diminishing returns. The effort it takes to make something better might not be worth the effort it takes to make that something better, if indeed it can be better.

Today's affirmation centers around a different result. With a little extra effort, something that is satisfactory can be made good and something that is good could be made great with a little effort.

The secret is to know the difference between something that is not worth the extra time, effort, and/or expense to be made great and something that with a little extra effort, or minimal effort, could be made great. My wife laughs at me for edging the sidewalk, driveway, and street curb. We enjoy working to make our lawn a lush green. What good is a masterpiece without having a beautiful frame around it? That little effort takes our yard from good to great.

Where can you apply a little extra effort today to make what is good *great*? In your job? Your relationships? The choice between good and great is yours.

Rewrite the affirmation three times:

1. _____

2. _____

3. _____

Personal thoughts:

_____

_____

_____

_____

_____

_____

_____

_____

_____

_____

Day 83

My goals end when I complete them, not when I tire of them.

Picture this scenario: You have a child who is a senior in college getting ready to start her final semester before graduation. She is a premed student with a 4.0 GPA. She tells you while home for Christmas break that she has decided to drop out of college and start a rock band. What do you say to her?

Now picture this scenario: Your father is three-quarters through cancer treatment and all indications show the cancer will be in remission. Dad then springs on you that he is done with all treatments and wants to buy an RV and tour the country. What do you say to him?

Chances are you know exactly what you would say to both your daughter and your father. They are too close to the finish line. They should complete what they started and then decide what to do next. Why is it that we have all the answers for when someone else wants to quit, but when we decide to throw in the towel before one of our goals are met, we have a thousand excuses why our choice is acceptable? If we truly want to quit a goal simply because we are tired of the effort to complete it, we must ask ourselves if we really wanted it in the first place.

Right now, assuming you have a goal set up for yourself and it is not yet complete, develop a strategy for when you tire of the goal prior to completion. This is extremely important because it will happen. In any marathon, fatigue will set in. Goal achievement is no different. What makes someone complete a marathon or complete a goal is the plan they have in place at the very beginning for when they tire of the goal prior to completion. Your goal ends at completion and not before.

Rewrite the affirmation three times:

1. _____

2. _____

3. _____

Personal thoughts:

_____

_____

_____

_____

_____

_____

_____

_____

_____

_____

Day 84

I have the power to say **no** *to temptation.*

Perhaps I should add "with the exception of chocolate" to this affirmation. Think about the word *temptation* for a minute. Is being tempted ever a good thing? Perhaps. Temptations almost always infer doing something that is not good for us. In previous affirmations, we focused on the word *power*, meaning control, might, etc. This affirmation means *you* have the control, the strength to avoid temptation.

What is the secret to being able to say no to temptation? The answer is simply knowing you will experience temptation and to be prepared for when it strikes. We prepare for many things in life. We prepare to go on vacation. We prepare to host a party at our home. Heck, we even prepare our responses to an upcoming, unpleasant conversation with someone. Being prepared means something is coming our way and we want to be ready to handle it. I've got news for you—temptation is coming your way! So let's be prepared when it arrives.

Let's do a little introspection here, a little self-examination with no one looking over your shoulder or into your head. In what areas of your life do you face the most temptation? Is it dietary? Is it financial? Is it internet related? Truthfully, it doesn't even matter. Temptation is temptation. If we want to have the power to say no to temptation, we must first recognize the areas we are most tempted in and try to avoid situations that lead to temptation. But if they are unavoidable, have a plan already in place that gives you the power to say *no!*

Rewrite the affirmation three times:

1. _____

2. _____

3. _____

Personal thoughts:

_____

_____

_____

_____

_____

_____

_____

_____

_____

_____

Day 85

What I put into life is more important than what I get out of life.

Let's visualize a long-term retirement account. For example, a person at age twenty started investing regularly, albeit conservatively, in the stock market. Through the miracle of compound interest, by the time they are ready to retire, the value of their portfolio will far surpass their actual dollars invested.

Our lives follow the same principle. What we put into life is far more important than what we get out. How can this be? In the stock market analogy, our net worth is greater at the end than what we put into it, so wouldn't what we get out be more important? No. If the person above were to never put a dime into their retirement account, they would have zero savings at the end. Likewise, if we put zero into life, at the end we will have gotten zero out of it. That is why what we put into life is more important than what we get out of it. Nothing *in* means nothing *out*.

How can we put more into life? First, be present in the moment. Whether you are with someone or simply resting, be 100 percent in that moment. Secondly, put more into life by simply living with an attitude of gratitude. When we are grateful, our lives become exponentially enhanced. Lastly, look to be of service wherever you are. If we simply look outside of ourselves to the world around us, we will find someone or something that needs a little caring.

Seek to fully understand that what we put into life is far more important than what we get out of life. The math does not lie.

Rewrite the affirmation three times:

1. _____

2. _____

3. _____

Personal thoughts:

_____

_____

_____

_____

_____

_____

_____

_____

_____

Day 86

I focus on what I have instead of what I do not have.

In a previous affirmation, we discussed being content with what we have but never being content with who we are. In other words, it was about letting go of the need to relentlessly pursue bigger and better material possessions (though there is nothing wrong with owning them) and continuously seeking to better ourselves as people instead. This affirmation is more about focusing on the intangibles of our lives, the things we take for granted when we long for other things.

There are many areas in our lives where we long for or focus on things we wish we had. A single person who is in one bad relationship after another might long for that one special person to come into their lives. Another person who has a good job might constantly dream about a different job. A couple might long for children, while other parents yearn for an empty nest.

Think how much happier we would be if we focused on the things we do have in life. Instead of focusing on getting older and a few more aches and pains, why don't I focus on our wonderful marriage, the four grown children who are doing well, and the five amazing grandchildren we have?

It is okay to want more for our lives, but the price of taking for granted and ignoring what is already good in our lives is too high. What in your life are you blessed with and can focus on right now? There are sure to be many things. How much different would our lives be if we spent more time focused on what is good in our lives and minimalized thinking of what is missing?

Rewrite the affirmation three times:

1. —————————————————————————————

2. —————————————————————————————

3. —————————————————————————————

Personal thoughts:

—————————————————————————————

—————————————————————————————

—————————————————————————————

—————————————————————————————

—————————————————————————————

—————————————————————————————

—————————————————————————————

—————————————————————————————

—————————————————————————————

Day 87

I think twice before communicating once.

The well-known carpenter's mantra is "measure twice, cut once." This is done both to save time from having to do the job again and to save money from wasting a piece of lumber. If there is a silver lining in this mantra, it is that if a mistake is made, it can be corrected. But there is a huge difference between that mantra and our affirmation for today. If we communicate without thinking, there is a good chance it may cause irreparable harm to others and to ourselves.

Unless you have lived your entire adult life on an uninhabited island, chances are you have communicated something that you later regretted. Perhaps you felt regret the instant the words left you. I am not writing solely about the spoken word: we often communicate regrettable things via social media, texts, emails, and any other means of communication.

It is obvious why we need to think twice before communicating once. Why don't we do this on a regular basis? There could be several reasons, but usually the prime suspect is emotional. It could be anger, hurt, sadness, and more. Other reasons for not thinking twice before communicating once are that we do not have all the information needed and we jump to conclusions.

The adage about counting to ten before reacting is true. Whereas cutting a piece of wood is easily correctable, how and what we communicate can have devasting consequences. Let us all think twice before communicating once.

Rewrite the affirmation three times:

1. _____

2. _____

3. _____

Personal thoughts:

_____

_____

_____

_____

_____

_____

_____

_____

_____

Day 88

I concentrate on being mentally strong.

This is an affirmation that I need to read daily. From time to time, I have dealt with mental health issues. Not being the sharpest tool in the box, it took me a long time to realize that being mentally strong is *not* the equivalent of never showing sadness, never allowing anyone else in, or not seeking help when needed. To be mentally strong means to allow all those things and more. It also requires concentration because it is easy to journey down the rabbit hole of mental illness without realizing it's happening until you've arrived.

In the past, I never wanted to appear weak in anything. If I had major surgery on a Friday, I would be back at work on Monday. If I had wisdom teeth taken out in the morning, I was at my desk in the afternoon.

I did the same thing with my mental health. I would smile when sad. When others offered to help me through some mentally trying time, I would shake them off as not needed. In my mind, to accept help was to be weak. As it turns out, not wanting to *appear* weak made me *mentally* weak. It wasn't until I mentally broke down that I made the connection that to be mentally strong was to be mentally healthy. Being mentally healthy and strong means to not be afraid to ask for help when needed. It means showing vulnerability. It means allowing people to see the real us and then permitting them to help us. That is mental strength.

Don't be like I used to be. We must recognize that being mentally strong means being mentally healthy . . . and we cannot accomplish it isolated on an island.

Rewrite the affirmation three times:

1. _____

2. _____

3. _____

Personal thoughts:

_____

_____

_____

_____

_____

_____

_____

_____

_____

Day 89

I harvest in direct proportion to what I sow.

There is a reason why most of the farmers in the world are part of huge conglomerates. To make a living, they must sow in massive quantities. Not only must they sow in enormous quantities, but they must also be selective in the seeds they sow.

The same principle applies to our lives. We harvest in direction proportion to what and how much we sow. If we desire love, kindness, compassion, and joy in our lives, we must sow many seeds of love, kindness, compassion, and joy. Additionally, when we sow these seeds, it cannot be a one-time thing. We must sow those seeds everywhere we go.

We all know people, either personally or by hearing about them, that cause us to say, "Man! I wish I could be like her." There are "Mother Teresas" all around us. As I write this, we are in the middle of the COVID-19 pandemic. I see the overwhelmed health care providers and marvel at what they do. The seeds they are sowing in the lives of others will produce a huge harvest, not only for their patients but in their own lives too.

Sadly, there are people who never sow any type of good seed, or worse, they sow seeds of evil. They, too, will harvest in direct proportion to what they sow.

Just writing this inspires me to sow good seeds wherever I go. And like any harvest, it may take a season before the reaping starts, but it will begin. Remember, we all harvest in direct proportion to what and how much we sow.

Rewrite the affirmation three times:

1. _____

2. _____

3. _____

Personal thoughts:

_____

_____

_____

_____

_____

_____

_____

_____

_____

_____

Day 90

I may be at the end of my rope, but I still have hope.

When I first wrote this affirmation, I had to chuckle because an image of the cartoon characters Wile E. Coyote and the Road Runner came into my head. Of course, Wile E. Coyote would fall, and the Road Runner would say, "Meep! Meep!" and speed away. But guess what? Wile E. Coyote would be back on the next episode. He always had hope.

Being at the end of our rope means that we have hit rock bottom—we cannot take any more. We are not able to deal with a person, a situation, or something else any longer. Have you ever been at the end of your rope? I know I have. If you are there, it is time to celebrate.

Why should we celebrate being at the end of our rope? At the end of our rope is hope. For most people, it isn't until we've reached the end of our ropes that we decide to make changes in our lives, changes that will enhance our lives. When we are sick and tired of being sick and tired, we will make changes to our health habits. When we are fed up with more month at the end of the money, we will make changes in our financial situation. I remember the last time as an adult that I asked to borrow money from my dad. He lent it, at 10 percent interest, but I remember thinking to myself, "That is it! Never again!" It was at that point that I made changes to how I increased income and cut spending, and that gave me hope.

Embrace being at the end of your rope if that is where you are. Changes, good changes, are coming your way.

Rewrite the affirmation three times:

1. _____

2. _____

3. _____

Personal thoughts:

_____

_____

_____

_____

_____

_____

_____

_____

_____

Day 91

I see things that may not be visible at this time.

I think we all have this attribute when it pertains to someone else, especially our children. Our lived experiences allow us to see things in our children's lives that they cannot see. For example, we can see how the choices our children make as teens are going to affect them later in life. As a managing broker for a real estate firm, I could tell within the first sixty days whether a new licensee was going to make it in this demanding industry.

Why don't we have this same capability when it pertains to ourselves and our own actions? Do we think we are above it all? Do we think we are smart enough that we absolutely know what we are doing, regardless of what people with more expertise or experience think?

I see things that may not be visible because I have learned to lean on the counsel of others. It does not matter if they are younger than me, or if they have a different background than I do. No man or woman is an island. In some cultures, people revere their elders. They count on them for guidance so they can see what is currently invisible. In our country, we tend to put the elderly out to pasture with words like, "They don't understand. Times are different now."

I encourage you to find people who know more than you do regarding various facets of life. Or find people who were once in the same position you are in right now. Listen, learn, and appreciate these people. They will help you see what is not visible at this time.

Rewrite the affirmation three times:

1. _____

2. _____

3. _____

Personal thoughts:

_____

_____

_____

_____

_____

_____

_____

_____

_____

Day 92

I focus on the goal and not the struggle to achieve it.

In your mind, picture the thoroughbred leading the race at the Kentucky Derby. Get a good image of that horse out front while the other horses are close behind. Now I ask you, have you ever seen a horse in this position, or any other position for that matter, turn their head and see who is behind or beside them? Hmm. The jockey may do this, but the horse never does. Why? Because the horse is focused on the goal and not on the struggle surrounding it.

We need to be like that winning horse. As we go through life trying to achieve goals we have set for ourselves, obstacles will appear. Forces are going to materialize that are in direct conflict with our goals. If we turn our focus to these outside forces and take our eyes off the goal, it will delay us from achieving our objective or perhaps even prevent it. Again, picture that winning horse.

We should expect opposition to our personal goals in life. This is important. If we expect opposition, even though we don't know where it will come from, we can prepare for it, defeat it, and remain focused on our goal. When the United States first put a man on the moon in 1969, do you think there was opposition? Do you think there were forces that threatened that mission? Did it keep NASA from reaching their goal?

We must know in our hearts and in our minds that we will experience struggles as we pursue our goals. To think otherwise is foolish. The key to achieving your goal is to remain focused on it, and not on the struggles. Can you do that?

Rewrite the affirmation three times:

1. _____

2. _____

3. _____

Personal thoughts:

_____

_____

_____

_____

_____

_____

_____

_____

_____

_____

Day 93

I value myself and avoid overvaluing myself.

Value refers to worth, usefulness, desirability, importance, significance, etc. To over-value something means to overrate, overestimate, and exaggerate. The term *overvalue* is often used in the stock market to indicate that the price of a stock is higher than what the stock is worth.

It is extremely important to value ourselves. Though most of us at some point in our lives feel like we do not have worth or desirability, it is important to fully understand that we are important. We are significant. People need us and that makes us useful. Our self-esteem rides largely on how we value ourselves. From our self-esteem comes our confidence. There is so much riding on how we value ourselves when it comes to mental health.

Some of us mistakenly overvalue ourselves. By overvaluing, we tend to exaggerate and overestimate our worth. Look around the world. When a famous athlete retires or goes to another team, does their former team collapse? When someone you work with takes another job, does their previous business collapse? When a family member unexpectedly passes away, does the family cease to exist? The answer to those questions is a resounding *no!*

You *are* valued! Today, make it a point to hang around people who value you. As a bonus, go out of your way to let someone else know that you value them. I promise that if we spend more time telling and showing others how much we value them, we will never overvalue ourselves.

Rewrite the affirmation three times:

1. _____

2. _____

3. _____

Personal thoughts:

_____

_____

_____

_____

_____

_____

_____

_____

_____

Day 94

I am teachable, and I am coachable.

Some people think these words are interchangeable, but there is a big difference between being teachable and being coachable. If we sincerely want to do well in whatever we choose to do, we need to understand and be both.

What does it mean to be teachable? It means we are capable of being taught something new. Children in school are teachable. Given the proper materials and instruction, they can be taught how to read, write, answer math equations, etc. People are taught how to drive a car, play music, and more. Being teachable means that you have the capacity to learn something new to you.

Being coachable means that you are willing to take knowledge that you already have and improve upon it to make a skill set better. We see coaches all around us. There are the obvious coaches in sport. Then we see a relatively new type of coach called a life coach who teaches people how to have more fulfilling lives. There are also business coaches. I remember hiring a coach to help me develop more business in real estate. I was very good at managing existing business but was weak in the development aspect of the profession, so I hired a coach to help me.

While being teachable and coachable are two different things, they both require one thing. They require that a person be *willing* to be taught something new and *willing* to be coached in what they already know. We all have weaknesses in our lives. Are you willing to be taught something, and then are you willing to be coached into doing it better or more effectively?

Rewrite the affirmation three times:

1. _____

2. _____

3. _____

Personal thoughts:

_____

_____

_____

_____

_____

_____

_____

_____

_____

Day 95

I value and cherish interdependence.

This affirmation is a tough one for me because I know intellectually that it is 100 percent true, but there are so many times in my life that I just want to run away and become a hermit. I desire no phone, no internet, no people—just me and nature. Have you ever felt that way? It is precisely for these occasional feelings that I value and cherish interdependence. People need other people and, believe it or not, we also need to be needed.

When we are teenagers, what it the one thing we want most, besides a vehicle on our sixteenth birthday? We want our independence, or at least we think we do. What we really want is to be free from our parents' control over our lives while still needing the shelter, food, and clothing they provide. But do parents need children? Of course, they do. Children fulfill so many intangible needs for parents, including the need to be needed. Remember, interdependence means people or countries depend on each other. Children *complete* parents as much as they *need* parents.

As we mature in life, it becomes more apparent that we not only need interdependence, but we also need to cherish it. We were created to be in fellowship with each other. Personally speaking, my darkest days happen when I seek to go it alone in life, when I simply want to run away from it all. Fortunately, the need for fellowship is in us all, so when I feel this way, those around me recognize it and rally to my rescue. With every day that passes, we all need to value and cherish our interdependence.

Rewrite the affirmation three times:

1. _____

2. _____

3. _____

Personal thoughts:

_____

_____

_____

_____

_____

_____

_____

_____

_____

Day 96

I am not defined by what others think of me.

I am me, and I am unique. Yes, I am flawed, but each day I try to improve myself. For many of us, we are defined by others by a single component or a combination of factors like our profession, past mistakes, past successes, finances (good or bad), family name, or religious affiliation. This is such a fallacy because the word *define* means to identify essential qualities, who we are intrinsically. All those other viewpoints are external and are a result of actions or circumstances. We must avoid thinking who we are is based on what others think we are.

How do you define yourself and should you even attempt to define yourself? If we define ourselves, are we putting ourselves into a similar box that others put us into? Do we limit our potential by doing so? What do I think of others? Am I comparable to the rest of the world and guilty of defining who people are based on the criteria in the first paragraph? That is so easy to do.

I believe that I do want to define myself, but not by any external measures. I want to define myself as a person whose nature seeks to become a better person to those around him, regardless of who they are. I desire to define myself as a person who takes action to make the world a better place. If I can create that legacy, even in my own mind, it will not matter what other people think about me.

Disregard how others define you, good or bad, as it is wrong and simply does not matter. The only thing that does matter is what we think of ourselves and how we can become a better person today than we were yesterday.

Rewrite the affirmation three times:

1. _____

2. _____

3. _____

Personal thoughts:

_____

_____

_____

_____

_____

_____

_____

_____

_____

_____

Day 97

I make wise choices regarding my time management.

We all use time management. What differentiates between a person who excels in it and a person who does not? There are two important skills pertaining to time management that, if used even partially, will greatly enhance anyone's use of time.

The first is the ability to simply say no. So many people are vying for our time outside of our commitments to family and work. These requests on our time relate to anything from volunteering to recreation. We often hear that it will only be one meeting per month, or that our skillset is desperately needed and without us the mission will fail. Or we hear, "It will only be for a couple of hours, and you deserve some fun." Face it, people like to please other people, so we often say yes to something when we should say no. When we fail to say no, we often add additional stress to our lives, and then our families and professions suffer too. We must learn to say no without experiencing guilt.

The other important skill is to recognize how precious our time is. We must use this very minute to get what needs to be done now, but also, if possible, things that need to be done down the road. We must use whatever time we can to work ahead in our list of to-dos. By doing so, when someone does ask us for some of our time, or something unexpected pops up, we are more able to say yes with no negative repercussions.

Learn to say no and learn to keep ahead of your to-dos. By doing so, you too will make wise choices regarding your time management.

Rewrite the affirmation three times:

1. _____

2. _____

3. _____

Personal thoughts:

_____

_____

_____

_____

_____

_____

_____

_____

_____

Day 98

I know my advantage in life is that I care for others.

Having an advantage in life is defined as having a favorable or superior position. It is up to the individual to determine their advantage in life. For some, it could be their family wealth. For others, it could be their educational level. Still others believe it is their work ethic. All of these are advantages, and there is absolutely nothing wrong with any of them. What is your advantage in life?

I seek to make my biggest advantage in life my care for others. When we genuinely care for others, it takes our minds off whatever is not quite right in our own world. If you could say that you have only a few troubles in life, wouldn't you agree that you have a tremendous advantage?

Caring for others can take many forms. Sure, there are tangible ways to show we care, but the most powerful way we can show someone we care is by sharing our most valuable personal asset—our time. When we take the time to listen, chat, exhort, and uplift another, it has a powerful impact. Not only does the person being cared for feel better, but this act of fellowship makes us feel better too. Any act of caring is good, but the best ones involve one-on-one fellowship.

Today, connect with someone to show them you care. Don't make it a touch-and-go gesture, but instead let them really know and feel that they are cared for. It will make a world of difference in both their and your life.

Rewrite the affirmation three times:

1. _____

2. _____

3. _____

Personal thoughts:

_____

_____

_____

_____

_____

_____

_____

_____

_____

Day 99

I am engaged in lifelong learning.

There are several reasons why I am engaged in lifelong learning. First, I love to learn, especially through formal academia. Engaging with other students or teachers is exhilarating. And the fact that I am in my sixties and learning purely for enjoyment and not necessity makes it even better.

The second reason I am engaged in lifelong learning is that I am trying to protect my mind. My father retired when he was sixty-five. He retired not only from work but from engaging in life. He sat in his chair from morning to night watching a far-leaning cable news channel. After a couple of years, our father, the patriarch of our family, who knew so much and who could repair anything, had a brain that had turned to mush. He walked three to five miles per day so that helped him have a healthy physical body, but he still had a brain of mush.

Our bodies need nourishment from the time we are in the womb until we take our last breath. Doesn't it make sense that our brains need nourishment during this same period? It is critical that as we age, we continue to feed our minds to avoid the natural tendency to lose brain function. Our physical bodies need exercise. So does our brain. Many people of advancing age resort to solving puzzles. That is fantastic. My preference is learning something new and then remembering it long enough to take a test.

Engage and commit yourself to lifelong learning. How cool is it to keep both our bodies and minds sharp at any age! Then we can take on the youngsters!

Rewrite the affirmation three times:

1. _____

2. _____

3. _____

Personal thoughts:

_____

_____

_____

_____

_____

_____

_____

_____

_____

_____

Day 100

I maintain integrity when I fulfill promises to myself and others.

How appropriate that this is the final affirmation in this book. As I type this, real tears are in my eyes because I started this book years ago. Back then, people knew I wrote daily affirmations. I boldly promised others and myself that one day I was going to write a book of my favorites, with stories and lessons regarding each one. Often, people would ask how I was progressing, and all I could say was that I was still working on it. With this page, I maintain my integrity by fulfilling my promise to myself and others.

I am glad I decided to publish this book, not just for myself, but for the people whom it will help. Over the decades, I have come to realize that my own mind is my worst enemy. It is only when I learn to control my thoughts that I can live the life I am meant to live. I hope you realize this as well.

If you are reading this, hopefully this book helped you too. Maybe there is something going on in your life that resonated with one of the affirmations. That is a good thing.

Integrity is priceless. Integrity or lack of integrity equals our reputation. In professional or personal life, our reputation for integrity sets us apart and above others. I want to conclude this final affirmation by asking you what promises you have made to yourself. What promises have you made to others? My wish for you is to rethink those promises and if they can be kept, go ahead and keep them. If they cannot be kept, let people know. I am rooting for you . . . I promise!

Rewrite the affirmation three times:

1. _____

2. _____

3. _____

Personal thoughts:

_____

_____

_____

_____

_____

_____

_____

_____

_____

_____

ACKNOWLEDGMENTS

First and foremost, I would like to thank God for the inspiration to help others through the writing of this book. Looking back at over sixty years of living, I am simply amazed at how he has protected me, provided for me, and loved me, most times without me even knowing it, let alone appreciating it.

I would also like to thank my bride of many years, Teresa. Her encouragement and self-sacrifice while I worked on this book, school, or whatever "squirrel" caught my eye are greatly appreciated. Without Teresa, this book would never have come to fruition. I love her with all my heart.

I would not be where I am today without the love and support of my children, Laura, Kate, Leigh, and Greg. Whether they knew it or not, watching them grow inspired me to be a better father, husband, and man. I wanted them to see what it was like to be a successful adult. They inspired me to be a better person.

Professionally speaking, Liz Moore and Mike Ferry were the catalysts to my professional success in real estate. Liz had faith in me as a rookie Realtor and took me under her wing to demonstrate to me that when we take care of the needs of our clients first, all of our needs will be taken care of as well. Mike Ferry was a huge contributor to my success, though he would not know me if I stood right next to him. It was through his company's training, seminars, and coaching that I learned the art of scheduling, and more importantly, surrounding yourself with good people and filling your mind with good thoughts. It was through Mike that I learned the power of affirmations.

ABOUT THE AUTHOR

With over forty years of leadership and management experience, both as a United States Air Force officer and real estate broker, **Robert "Sully" Sullivan** has not only witnessed and coached others through the daily ups and downs of life—he has experienced them himself. Decades ago, Sullivan decided to fill his mind with positive, uplifting reading (both secular and spiritual) at the start of each day. The more he filled his mind with positive affirmations, the better his life became, and when he strayed from those positive influences, his mental health declined. Through his speaking and writing, he encourages others to take charge of their mindset to live a better life. He lives with his wife Teresa in Virginia.

TOPICAL INDEX

TIME

POWER OF VISION

POWER OF THOUGHTS

Day 22: I have the power to choose so I also have the power to change.

Day 25: I have taken charge of who I am.

Day 35: I have stopped the negative chatter in my brain.

Day 36: I seek to be the lit candle in a dark room.

Day 37: I seek out ways to praise and encourage others.

Day 38: I work hard to protect my heart, mind, and soul.

Day 44: I am careful not to think or speak ill of others.

Day 60: I have eliminated the emotional debris from my head.

Day 66: I avoid having irritations ruin my day.

Day 77: I recognize every moment is a precious gift.

Day 81: I live life with an attitude of gratitude.

Day 86: I focus on what I have instead of what I don't have.

POWER OF ACTION AND HABITS

Day 3:   I remind myself daily of the person I wish to be.

Day 7:   I always work ten minutes more when I feel like quitting.

Day 19: I take time to review my daily habits and actions.

Day 21: I am the blacksmith of my life.

Day 40: I know what is important in my life.

Day 49: I know the longer I carry a problem, the heavier it gets.

Day 50: I know the cost of my future is based on the price I pay today.

Day 52: I change today so tomorrow will be better than yesterday.

Day 53: I understand the power of vision plus intentional action.

Day 57: I transform great ideas into great action.

Day 61: I approach each task as if my legacy depends on it.

Day 74: I have taken charge of my life.

GROWTH MINDSET

Day 1:   I renew my spirit and mindset every day.

Day 8:   I am willing to start at the beginning.

Day 17: I do not pursue happiness; I create it.

VALUE OF ADVERSITY, RISKS, AND MISTAKES

Day 78: I embrace rejection as it is a growth opportunity.

Day 90: I may be at the end of my rope, but I still have hope.

RELATIONSHIPS

Day 15: I focus on the people I am talking to.

Day 16: I choose great people to be around.

Day 37: I seek out ways to praise and encourage others.

Day 44: I am careful not to think or speak ill of others.

Day 68: I am fully engaged with the people I am with.

Day 71: I seek to be a moment of joy in the lives of others.

Day 75: I have let go of unrealistic expectations and their stress.

Day 79: I polish my marriage daily.

Day 87: I think twice before communicating once.

Day 95: I value and cherish interdependence.

GRIT/DETERMINATION

Day 3:   I remind myself daily of the person I wish to be.

Day 6:   I know my success starts the moment I do.

Day 7:   I always work ten minutes more when I feel like quitting.

Day 8:   I am willing to start at the beginning.

Day 9:   I know that triumph lies in discipline.

Day 10: I give myself freedom to fail.

Day 12: I row where there is no wind.

Day 38: I work hard to protect my heart, mind, and soul.

Day 45: I am rededicated to the priorities of my life.

Day 61: I approach each task as if my legacy depends on it.

Day 62: I strive for what is just beyond my grasp.

Day 63: I wholeheartedly give myself to this day.

Day 67: I persevere long after the others have quit.

Day 69: I succeed because I am willing to succeed.

Day 83: My goals end when I complete them, not when I tire of them.

Day 92: I focus on the goal and not the struggle to achieve it.

PERSONAL RESPONSIBILITY AND INTEGRITY

Day 18: I control my life; it is not on autopilot.

Day 23: I know personality opens doors, but character keeps them open.

Day 29: I am a faithful steward of my resources.

Day 39: I do the job right the first time, so I do not have to do it again.

Day 42: I have a passion for success that is stronger than my fear of failure.

Day 51: I live my life in a manner I wish my children to live theirs.

Day 54: I am kind even if others would understand if I wasn't.

Day 55: I judge each day by the seeds I plant and those I nurture.

Day 61: I approach each task as if my legacy depends on it.

Day 62: I strive for what is just beyond my grasp.

Day 63: I wholeheartedly give myself to this day.

Day 64: I survive both adversity and prosperity.

Day 72: I strive to be who I want my children to be.

Day 82: I know the difference between good and great is a little effort.

Day 84: I have the power to say no to temptation.

Day 89: I harvest in direct proportion to what I sow.

Day 100: I maintain integrity when I fulfill promises to myself and others.

GIVING/SERVICE

Day 26: I am creating enough evidence to be convicted of being kind.

Day 28: I know where I can make a difference, so I do.

Day 30: I am specific when I offer to help.

Day 41: I know the impact that service to others has on my joy.

Day 59: To get what I need, I must first help someone get what they need.

Day 70: I get my greatest joy when I serve others.

Day 80: I cannot do everything, but I can do something.

Day 98: I know my advantage in life is that I care for others.

FAITH/PROVIDENCE

Day 20: I work on my weaknesses instead of others' weaknesses.

Day 31: I am content with my surroundings but not with myself.

Day 38: I work hard to protect my heart, mind, and soul.

Day 49: I know the longer I carry a problem, the heavier it gets.

FINANCES

Day 56: I anticipate problems and then address them before they arrive.

Day 62: I strive for what is just beyond my grasp.

Day 64: I survive both adversity and prosperity.

A free ebook edition is available with the purchase of this book.

To claim your free ebook edition:

1. Visit MorganJamesBOGO.com
2. Sign your name CLEARLY in the space
3. Complete the form and submit a photo of the entire copyright page
4. You or your friend can download the ebook to your preferred device

A **FREE** ebook edition is available for you or a friend with the purchase of this print book.

_____

CLEARLY SIGN YOUR NAME ABOVE

Instructions to claim your free ebook edition:
1. Visit MorganJamesBOGO.com
2. Sign your name CLEARLY in the space above
3. Complete the form and submit a photo of this entire page
4. You or your friend can download the ebook to your preferred device

Print & Digital Together Forever.

Snap a photo

Free ebook

Read anywhere

CPSIA information can be obtained
at www.ICGtesting.com
Printed in the USA
JSHW081713230623
43678JS00001B/54